USDA
United States Department of Agriculture

I0410343

Direct Seeding Southern Pines: History and Status of a Technique Developed for Restoring Cutover Forests

James P. Barnett

Forest Service
Research & Development
Southern Research Station
General Technical Report SRS-187

The Author:

James P. Barnett, retired Chief Silviculturist
and Emeritus Scientist, U.S. Department of
Agriculture Forest Service, Southern Research
Station, Pineville, LA 71360.

Cover: Harold J. Derr, research forester for the Southern Forest Experiment Station, Pineville, LA, sowing longleaf pine seeds with a cyclone seeder in 1954. Derr was a leader in the development of direct seeding technology.

Photo credits: Unless otherwise noted, the photographs are from collections of the U.S. Forest Service. Many of the photographs were taken by contract photographers, Elmore Morgan and Tommy Kohara.

Product Disclaimer

The use of trade or firm names in this publication is for reader information and does not imply endorsement by the U.S. Department of Agriculture of any product or service.

Pesticide Precautionary Statement

This publication reports research involving pesticides. It does not contain recommendations for their use, nor does it imply that the uses discussed here have been registered. All uses of pesticides must be registered by appropriate State and/or Federal agencies before they can be recommended. CAUTION: Pesticides can be injurious to humans, domestic animals, desirable plants, and fish or other wildlife—if they are not handled or applied properly. Use all pesticides selectively and carefully. Follow recommended practices for the disposal of surplus pesticides and pesticide containers.

Conversions

1 acre = 0.40 hectare	1 fluid ounce = 29.6 milliliters
1 foot = 30.5 centimeters	1 pound = 0.45 kilograms
1 inch = 2.54 centimeters	1 tablespoon = 14.8 milliliters
1 bushel = 0.035 cubic meters	1 gallon = 3.78 liters

January 2014

Southern Research Station
200 W.T. Weaver Blvd.
Ashevile, NC 28804

www.srs.fs.usda.gov

Direct Seeding Southern Pines: History and Status of a Technique Developed for Restoring Cutover Forests

James P. Barnett

PREFACE

For centuries, foresters throughout the World have been intrigued by the idea of establishing forest stands by sowing limited quantities of seeds at the right time on a suitable seedbed. Following the harvest of southern pine forests during the late 19th and early 20th centuries, the great need for reforestation in the South called for innovative ideas. Millions of acres of cutover forests lay decimated with no residual source of seed that could provide natural regeneration.

Pioneers in reforestation of southern pines conducted numerous trials of seeding, and although there were occasional successes, failures greatly outnumbered them. These early attempts did show, however, that the biggest obstacle to seeding was seed predation by birds and rodents.

Research on direct seeding began in 1947 by scientists of the Southern Forest Experiment Station located at Alexandria, LA. The objective of this research was to find a practical method of protecting seeds from birds, since resident and migratory species are numerous on these cutover areas when pine seeds were sown. Led by efforts of Harold J. Derr and William F. Mann, Jr., a breakthrough was found in 1953 when anthraquinone and an imported commercial repellent containing anthraquinone were found to be effective, nontoxic bird repellents.

A formulation of the fungicide thiram was found to be equally effective in protecting seeds from birds. By the end of 1957, a seed coating was tested that included thiram and endrin which repelled birds, rodents, and many insects. Pilot trials were undertaken immediately by industrial landowners, mostly in Louisiana where the research was conducted. The early operations were so successful that the technique soon was applied around the region, and within 10 years almost 1 million acres were directly seeded with southern pines.

The practice proved applicable in all parts of the South, and an intensive supporting research program began to provide the additional quantities of seed needed to control the many species of undesired, low-quality hardwoods that occupied many pine sites, and to determine the extent that site preparation practices were needed for successful seeding.

Direct seeding was highly effective in restoring southern pines to millions of acres of cutover forest land throughout the South. However, as much of the open forest land was regenerated by planting and seeding efforts, the need for direct seeding declined. Use of seeding is most appropriate on these large, open areas. Also, loss of the availability of endrin, an effective rodent repellent, further limited the application of seeding. The replacement rodent repellent, concentrated hot sauce or capsicum, is less effective than was endrin.

Although direct seeding is inexpensive compared to planting of bareroot nursery stock, it is frequently less successful and may require precommercial thinning of resulting overstocked stands. It is now used primarily to regenerate large forested areas destroyed by wildfire. It did, however, serve as a valuable application in response to the huge reforestation problem resulting from the deforestation of the South's pine lands during the late 19th and early 20th centuries.

James P. Barnett

CONTENTS

Direct Seeding Southern Pines: History and Status of a Technique Developed for Restoring Cutover Forests

James P. Barnett

Abstract

Early in the 20th century the deforestation resulting from the "golden-age of lumbering" left millions of acres of forest land in the need for reforestation. The challenge was so extreme that foresters of the early 1930s estimated that it would take 900 to 1,000 years at the then rate of planting to reforest the denuded forest land that occurred throughout the Nation. Forests of the West Gulf region were especially decimated due to the development and use of steam-powered logging equipment that left little capability for natural regeneration. Faced with this need, scientists of the Southern Forest Experiment Station began an effort to develop direct seeding with the hope of quickly seeding large open areas of the South with southern pines. Protecting seeds from bird and rodent predation was key to successful direct seeding, and in the mid-1950s certain chemicals were found that made seeding an effective tool. Additional components of a successful direct seeding operation were increasing the availability of quality pine seeds, finding methods of eliminating hardwood brush competition, and developing site preparation treatments that favored seeding. This supporting research was essential for the resulting successful restoration of millions of acres of southern pine forests. Today, direct seeding is infrequently used, primarily due to lack of large, open areas needing reforestation. But back then, seeding met a significant need, and millions of acres of forest land were put back into production.

Keywords: Chemical hardwood control, competition control, precommercial thinning, reforestation, seed repellents, seed research, site preparation, southern pines, stand stocking

THE NEED FOR DIRECT SEEDING TECHNOLOGY

Much of the up to 90 million acres of longleaf pine (*Pinus palustris*) occurring throughout the Coastal Plain of the South were harvested by aggressive logging in the late 1800s and early 1900s. The longleaf forests of the Western Gulf Coast region were particularly devastated by use of steam-powered logging equipment that was developed as the harvest of the forests of this region began. Railroads extending into the flat land of the upland pine forests brought log skidding and loading equipment that were very efficient, but destroyed nearly all non-merchantable trees as well as those harvested. This resulted in millions of acres of cutover forests without the seed sources needed for reforestation.

Steam-powered skidders manufactured by the Clyde Ironworks in Duluth, MN, greatly increased logging capability in the early 1900s.

In 1954, Philip C. Wakeley, a scientist with the Forest Service, U.S. Department of Agriculture estimated that 13 million acres across the South were currently in need of reforestation (Wakeley 1954). When the Alexandria Research Center (ARC) was established following World War II, the territory served by ARC covered over 7 million acres in central and southwestern Louisiana and east Texas. Almost 80 percent was commercial forest land and nearly half of that once supported magnificent stands of virgin longleaf pine. Over 20 percent (1,250,000 acres) was barren of pines, and another 3 million acres were much below full potential of the land because it was largely covered by scrub oaks and other low-value hardwoods (Cassidy and Mann 1954).

It was estimated that if the treeless longleaf pine land in Louisiana and Texas was reforested by planting nursery grown seedlings, the job would take 50 or more years at the rate feasible with the then current nursery capability (Cassidy and Mann 1954). There was a significant need to develop additional technology to meet this awesome reforestation project. Although expanding bareroot nursery capacity was an obvious goal, another option was development of a direct seeding capability.

EARLY SEEDING ATTEMPTS

Direct seeding had been considered for generations as a potential forest regeneration technique. The sowing of tree seeds on prepared forest soils was often considered and tried—and sometimes the trials met with success. Barnett (2011) describes Great Southern Lumber Company's hand seeding in 1920 of slash pine (*P. elliottii*) on furrows plowed by teams of mules. An 800-acre tract was successfully regenerated and is considered the first successful commercial direct seeding in the United States.

Great Southern Lumber Company's head ranger, F.O. "Red" Bateman, was responsible for this seeding operation. Other seeding trials were not successful, however, and Bateman was quoted as describing to young research foresters his evaluation of the potential of direct seeding:

When we went out to start seeding, there was a pheelock [field lark or meadowlark] sittin' on a fence, he whistled, and up come fifty more feellocks. We went down the furrows, dropping longleaf seeds every six feet. The pheelock follered us down the furrows, and, gentlemen, when we got to the end of the furrows, there wasn't a damn thing left in the furrows but bird-sh-t! (Wakeley 1976).

INITIATION OF A SEEDING RESEARCH PROGRAM

In 1946, the Southern Forest Experiment Station established the ARC in central Louisiana. The mission of the ARC was to develop improved methods of reforestation and management to guide landowners in the task of attaining optimum production and income from their forest land. When established, five areas of research were selected in consultation with the Center's Research Advisory Committee:

Top: Old-growth longleaf pine stands like this occupied about 90 million acres across the South's Coastal Plain when settlers arrived.
Bottom: This area became a part of the Palustris Experimental Forest and represented millions of acres of cutover forests across the South.

Top: In 1920, the Great Southern Lumber Company reforestation efforts began with this direct seeding of slash pine on sites created by plowing furrows. Bottom: This is the 800-acre slash pine plantation 5 years following direct seeding into furrows plowed by mules.

2

(1) Reforesting the cutover lands.
(2) Managing pine plantations for optimum returns.
(3) Controlling low-value hardwoods with chemicals.
(4) Improving management of livestock and forage on forest ranges.
(5) Determining costs and returns of good forest management.

Of these, the highest priority was in developing and improving techniques to reforest cutover pine lands (Cassidy and Mann 1954).

Derr (1958) justified the direct seeding effort based on four rationales. First, direct seeding was seen as fast and required minimum labor. He reasoned that one man with a planting tool could plant, if his back held out, 1 acre of pine seedlings per day. With a planting machine, he could plant 5 to 6 acres per day. But, with aerial seeding, a pilot could seed 1,000 acres in 1 day.

The second reason for seeding was that it was cheaper. While the cost fluctuated with cost of seed, it did not exceed $10 per acre. Planting seedlings cost at least twice that amount.

Third, seeding provided for denser stands—a result that was better for longleaf pine—than did planting of bareroot seedlings. While this later turned out to be an undesirable outcome, originally dense stands of longleaf seedlings were desired to overcome seedling losses during the grass stage of the species. Most longleaf pine sites to be reforested had a serious infestation of brown-spot needle blight (*Mycosphaerella dearnessii*, previously *Scirrhia acicola*) that remained from the earlier stands and resulted in significant seedling mortality. Direct seeding was seen as a significant new method for reforesting longleaf pine. In the early 1950s, <100 acres of longleaf pine seedlings were planted each year (Mann 1956).

Finally, direct seeding could be expanded quickly to take advantage of bumper seed crops. At that time, storage of longleaf pine seeds was problematic.

Because direct seeding promised to be cheaper, faster, and more efficient than planting, it became a major research project of the ARC. By 1954, about 3,000 acres in direct seeding experiments were conducted using longleaf, slash, and loblolly (*P. taeda*) pines. No successful method of application had been found, but the major causes of failure had been identified (Cassidy and Mann 1954).

Seed-eating birds, chiefly eastern meadowlarks (*Sturnella magna*) and field sparrows (*Spizella pusilla*) were the greatest problem. The vast areas of cutover forests provided

The cutover forests provided ideal habitat for flocks of eastern meadowlarks which ate huge quantities of seeds.

the ideal habitat for large flocks of these birds (Burleigh 1938). Research indicated that coating the seeds with a chemical repellent was a promising technique. Rodents, too, were predatory, but for fall-sown longleaf pine the menace was less than from the birds.

The direct seeding research initiative was led by Harold J. Derr and William F. Mann, Jr. Derr was the scientist assigned to the project, and Mann, who was the Center Leader, supervised and participated in the effort.

DEVELOPMENT OF REPELLANTS

Early in the evaluations of direct seeding, predator control by men patrolling with shot guns was the only practical method of reducing losses of seeds to birds—mostly large flocks of migrant species. A minimum of a one-man shotgun patrol was assigned to each 200 acres of seeding for at least 8 hours per day during the 5-week germination period. Even this expensive measure was not always effective (Mann 1956, Mann and Derr 1955).

Bird Repellents

In 1953 and 1954, tests began with a chemical bird repellent called Morkit® which was used to coat the seed (Mann and Derr 1955). Morkit® was manufactured in Germany and consisted of a mixture of anthraquinone and inert ingredients.

A cooperative effort between scientists of the ARC and U.S. Fish and Wildlife Service evaluated Morkit® and related anthraquinone compounds. Anthraquinone is environmentally safe and is used in numerous compounds such as dyes, laxatives, and cosmetic products. Previous tests evaluated other compounds and colored seed coatings, none of which were effective repellents for southern pine seeds.

Tests showed that seeds treated with Morkit® yielded 4,500 seedlings per acre, and untreated seeds only 195 (Mann and Derr 1955). In 1954, a large-scaled test of Morkit® and anthraquinone compounds showed them equally effective; each yielded about 3,000 seedlings per acre. Untreated seeds produced only about 250 seedlings per acre. Birds consumed 90 percent of the untreated seeds in 11 days.

Morkit® was withdrawn from the United States market in 1955 and additional tests with U.S. Fish and Wildlife Service scientists found that Arasan Seed Disinfectant and Protectant® (50 percent tetramethyl thiuram disulphide), now marketed as thiram, was equally effective as anthraquinone compounds in repelling birds (Meanley and others 1957). Caged tests determined that birds did not eat seeds treated with these chemicals and that the treatments stopped predation. Also, Mann and others (1956) noted that thiram had some rodent-repellent qualities. Because of the rodent repellency aspect of Arasan® (thiram), it replaced

Top: Harold J. Derr standing beside slash pine saplings established by direct seeding. **Bottom:** *Longleaf pine seeds treated with repellent coatings consisting of Arasan 75®, latex, and aluminum flakes.*

anthraquinone as the preferred seed treatment. It did, however, have some problems—it irritated the eyes, nose, and throat. It also had a negative effect on seed germination when laboratory tests were conducted in closed germination dishes.

Thiram 42-S®, a liquid formulation, later became the preferred formulation to use in direct seeding because it provided a durable, dust-free coating that was superior to any previous formulation (Mann 1970). It is also an effective, registered fungicide formulation frequently used as a seed treatment to control seedborne microorganisms and continues to be registered as a tree seed treatment for bird repellency.

Rodent Repellents

Although early studies found that birds were the primary predators of pine seeds, these tests were conducted with longleaf pine seeds sown in the fall (November and early December) on sites with a light grass rough (Derr 1958, Mann 1956). Longleaf seeds lack dormancy and germinate soon after natural dispersal in the fall. When more dormant seeds of pine species that require stratification were sown in the spring, they were found to be subject to heavy rodent predation because rodent populations increase during the winter and early spring.

As early as 1956, Mann (1956) found that seeds sown in late December and early spring needed protection from rodents. Cooperative studies with scientists of the U.S. Fish and Wildlife Service were conducted to find chemicals that would reduce the losses from rodents. Even though Arasan® provided some protection from rodents, adding the chemical endrin to the seed coating greatly improved seeding success when seeds were sown later in the winter (Derr and Mann 1959).

Endrin 50W®, sold mainly as an insecticide, was a potent chlorinated hydrocarbon poison and presented a hazard to the environment and animal life. All who used the chemical were required to wear a respirator and rubber gloves and change and wash their clothes daily. Although incorporating endrin into the repellent coating significantly increased seeding success, it caused concern because of its extreme toxicity. It typically was added to the other chemicals at a rate of 1 pound (0.5 pound active ingredient) per 100 pounds of seeds (Derr and Mann 1959, Mann 1958).

There was some question whether endrin was truly a repellent or if it killed the rodents that ate the seeds. Evaluations seemed to confirm the hypothesis that rodents ate some of the treated seeds, became sick, and then avoided continued predation. In the early 1970s, however, public concern about the use of many extremely toxic chemicals

James P. "Jim" Barnett led the cooperative effort to maintain the registration of endrin.

in agriculture caused the Environmental Protection Agency (EPA) and the U.S. Department of Agriculture (USDA) to begin a program to review the registration of such chemicals. Endrin was high on the list of chemicals to be reviewed and James P. Barnett of the ARC was selected to lead the multi-agency USDA team to conduct a benefit/risk assessment of the chemical.

The assessment recommended (Barnett and others 1977)—and the EPA accepted—continued use of endrin in forestry direct seeding primarily due to the small amount distributed to any acre of land during seeding. Other uses, which accounted for most of the market for the chemical, were generally not approved. As the result, although still registered by the EPA for the direct seeding application, the product was removed from the market in the United States by the manufacturer.

When availability of endrin ended, the use of direct seeding began to decline—large, open sites where its use was best suited were generally not available. So, although the need for a rodent repellent lessened, an effort was made to find a chemical with rodent repellency that could replace endrin. Campbell (1981a) and Barnett (1995) evaluated several possible chemicals, but none were found that were environmentally safe as well as effective.

More recently, field tests have shown that the substance oleoresin capsicum has promise as a rodent repellent (Barnett 1998). Capsicum is obtained from dried cayenne peppers (*Capsicum frutescens*) and is standardized with olive oil. The chemical in capsicum that can produce a burning sensation in the mouth is capsaicin. Its strength is measured in parts per million (ppm). The ppm are converted to Scoville Units (SV), the industry standard for measuring the heat of peppers (American Spice Trade Association 1960, Hoffman and Lego 1983). One ppm is equivalent to 15 SV. The material in this study had an SV of 500,000. Although capsicum is a natural and nontoxic chemical derived from pepper plants and is used in many foodstuffs to increase their pungency, it is an irritant to the skin and

eyes. Protective gloves and eyewear are recommended when using concentrated forms of this product.

Nolte and Barnett (2000) evaluated the efficacy of thiram-capsicum treatments to house (*Mus musculus*) and deer (*Peromyscus maniculatus*) mice that cause damage to longleaf pine seeds. The combination of thiram and capsicum was found to protect seeds from deer mice and is a potential repellent to protect pine seeds from rodent predation when used in direct seeding.

Chemicals to Aid Coating Applications

Another aspect of the collaboration with the U.S. Fish and Wildlife Service was to identify chemicals that could be used as a sticker for coating repellents on seeds. Early on, Flintkote C-13-HPC®, an asphalt emulsion, was found to effectively bind the coating material to seeds (Mann 1958). Additional studies found that Dow Latex 512-R® was equally effective (Mann 1959). The latex product soon became the one used routinely in repellent treatments because it could be more easily applied to seeds.

A germinated longleaf pine seed coated with the thiram-endrin repellent.

Forestry technician, Tommy Rhame, demonstrating seed treatment used early in the development of direct seeding.

Tommy Melder mixing latex into an Arasan-42S® repellent formulation.

Fifteen tablespoons of aluminum powder is typically applied to the repellent mixture for 100 pounds of seeds to increase the flow of the seeds through seed-sowing equipment (Derr and Mann 1959).

Seed Coating Techniques

Repellent treatments evolved over time. Early in the development of repellents, anthraquinone and Arasan® became effective treatments. These were applied as a powder formulation and at the rate of 15 percent by weight (15 pounds per 100 pounds of seeds); when Arasan-75® became available it could be used at 10 percent because of its higher concentration of active ingredients (Derr 1958). All of these treatments were applied as an overcoating after the seeds were immersed in an adhesive solution of either asphalt emulsion or latex in water.

The asphalt adhesive Flintkote C-13-HPC® was diluted in water with a ratio of 1:3, whereas Dow Latex 512-R® was mixed with water in the ratio of 1:9.

Repellents were evaluated over time and modified to take advantage of improved formulations. They were standardized using a water suspension of thiram marketed as Arasan-42S®, Dow Latex 512-R®, and Endrin-50W® (Derr and Mann 1971). The repellent mixture consists of 1 gallon of thiram, 5 fluid ounces of latex, and ½ pound of endrin. This mixture usually treats about 50 pounds of seeds, but the amount treated will vary by pine species. About 8 tablespoons of aluminum powder are typically added to ensure the flow of seeds through sowing equipment.

Once the seeds are treated they are spread on polyethylene sheeting to dry for about 30 minutes.

SEED QUALITY AND QUANTITY

A significant problem in the development of direct seeding as a forest regeneration technique was access to large quantities of pine seeds. This was particularly true for sowing longleaf pine seeds since there was lack of information on successfully collecting, processing, treating, and storing these seeds. Initially, longleaf pine seeds were thought to be viable only if freshly collected, so, availability of seeds was limited by the size of the annual cone crop.

Since research was needed to provide guidelines for seed production and storage, in 1957, Bobbie F. "Mac"

B.F. McLemore was hired to begin a research program in seed science that would support direct seeding and nursery research efforts.

McLemore was recruited to begin a research program in seed science. In 1961, James P. "Jim" Barnett was added to the staff to assist in the seed research program.

Procurement

Amounts of southern pine seeds were insufficient to meet increasing needs for direct seeding; therefore, many landowners began to collect cones for processing. As seed dealers became established, cone and seed processing was typically contracted.

Various questions related to cone collecting times, cone handling, and seed processing were addressed. Procurement of local sources of seeds was generally recommended, but with the infrequency of cone crops, seed zones began to be developed to provide guidance on appropriate locations for collection (Wells 1969). Studies that followed have provided collection guidelines for all major southern pines (Schmidtling 2001).

Establishment of forest seed dealers, such as the pioneering American Forest Seed Company (AFSC), provided a needed resource in meeting the needs for direct seeding. Howell Cobb of the AFSC developed early commercial collection, processing, treating, and storing services (Barnett 2011). The leadership of Derwood Delaney, the operations manager of the AFSC, later led to the development of the Louisiana Forest Seed Company, a premier forest seed provider (Barnett and Burns 2011).

Collection and Processing

The dilemma of inadequate amounts of quality longleaf pine seed, as well as for other southern pine species, resulted in creation of a seed research program of wide scope. The timing and location of cone collections and cone handling and processing techniques needed to maintain high seed quality were important issues to be resolved. Although

Derwood Delaney (center) with sons John (left) and Gary (right) provide a full range of forest seed capabilities through their Louisiana Forest Seed Company.

Wakeley (1954) had developed some cone maturity guidelines, the demand for huge quantities of seeds resulting from direct seeding required better data on timing of cone collection—both its initiation and length.

Estimating cone and seed production—Direct seeding and increasing nursery production required the production of large quantities of high quality seeds. Seed collectors needed methods to determine where and when to collect cones. A number of studies provided guidelines on how to provide early estimates of annual cone production. Techniques for such estimation were based on counting numbers of female flowers or strobili in the spring about 18 months before cone maturity (Croker 1971, Fatzinger and others 1988) and binocular counts of cones a few months before cone ripening (Wasser and Dierauf 1979, Webb and Hunt 1965, Wenger 1953). The counting of strobili provided less accurate predictions of cone production than estimates based on binocular counts of cones (Shoulders 1968).

Although knowing the size of the cone crop is important, equally significant is information on the seed yields per bushel of cones collected (Bramlett and Hutchinson 1964). This information allows collectors and buyers to estimate cone requirements before collection starts and concentrate picking in areas where seed yields are highest.

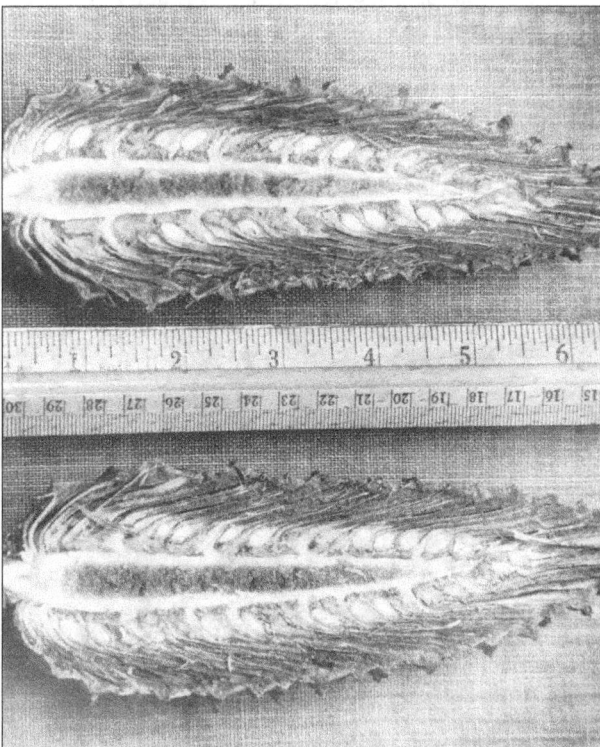

A sliced longleaf pine cone showing exposed seeds that become the basis for predicting the seed yields of southern pines.

The idea of cutting sample cones and counting exposed seeds as an index of seed yields had been suggested for many years (Hopkins 1956, Syverson 1960). McLemore (1961a) used the cone-cutting procedure to develop relationships between the numbers of seeds exposed by slicing and the total number of sound seeds per cone. With the additional information on the number of seeds per pound and number of cones per bushel, McLemore (1962) published methods for projecting seed yields per bushel of collected cones for longleaf, slash, and loblolly pine.

McLemore's techniques, summarized later by Barnett (1999), became widely used by seed dealers in determining where and when to make cone collections.

Cone specific gravity measurement—Specific gravity (SG), computed by dividing cone weight by the weight of water the cone displaces, is the most reliable method of determining cone maturity in southern pines. For decades, Wakeley's (1954) method of floating cones in SAE 20 motor oil (SG of 0.88) simplified cone specific gravity determinations. When cones floated in the oil, they had reached the point where their scales would open when collected and dried. Extension of the collection period became possible with lengthening cone storage times, but the need for a simple technique to measure SG was needed.

Barnett (1979a) published a simplified flotation procedure developed by B.F. McLemore for determining cone SG in the field. Graduated cylinders of a size to accommodate species differences in cone size are filled to a convenient level with water and the level noted. When a cone is added to the cylinder, the difference between the water levels provides a measurement of cone weight. If the cone sinks

Early cone collections were made by climbing trees and dislodging cones with a hooked pole.

the SG is greater than 1.0 and cannot be measured. The water level of floating cones submerged by a wire or small stick is noted. The difference between this and the initial level provides a measurement of cone volume. The division of cone weight by cone volume provides SG.

Cone/seed maturity relationships—Until seeds disperse from cones on trees, germination of longleaf pine seeds increases as cone specific gravity decreases (McLemore 1959). Once collected, longleaf seeds do not continue to mature in cone storage, and cone storage decreases seed viability unless collections are delayed until natural cone opening is imminent (Barnett 1976a). Even though seed yields increase with cone storage, storing cones more than 30 days reduces storability of the seeds (McLemore 1961b).

In contrast, viability of slash pine seeds continues to increase during storage of harvested cones if the cones are fully mature when picked. Loblolly pine seeds mature (will germinate) before seed yields indicate cones are ripe, and more than 95 percent of loblolly seeds are viable before they can be extracted. In order to obtain both optimum seed yield and seed quality, efforts to determine the relationship between indices of cone maturity and seed maturity were evaluated (Barnett 1976a, 1979b). These studies evaluating the relation of cone ripening and seed maturity provided the information needed to lengthen the cone collection period, and it was extended for all the major southern pine species.

Overcoming processing problems—Longleaf pine seeds are the most difficult of the southern pines to collect, process, store, and treat successfully. Because the seeds are large, have thin seedcoats, and are usually moist when extracted from cones, collecting and processing them without adversely affecting quality requires special handling procedures.

Ripening immature or holding mature longleaf cones before extraction may or may not improve seed viability (Barnett 1976a, Bonner 1987, McLemore 1975), but some cone storage is needed to improve seed yields (Barnett 1996).

During the processing stage, dewinging of longleaf seeds may adversely affect the quality of seeds extracted from mature cones. The possible causes of dewinging damage are lack of seed drying, inappropriate dewinging equipment, and large-sized seeds. Drying seed prior to dewinging results in more brittle wings that are quickly and easily reduced to stubs (Barnett 1996). However, excessive drying at high temperatures may also reduce seed quality.

Longleaf pine seeds require dewinging equipment designed for more sensitive seeds. Many tests have shown that the harshness and length of dewinging must be minimized. Equipment used for dewinging loblolly or slash pine

Longleaf pine cones collected and held in crates, awaiting processing.

Testing southern pine seeds for germination potential. (Photo courtesy of Weyerhaeuser Company)

is usually inappropriate for longleaf pine (Barnett and Pesacreta 1993).

Once dewinged and dried, longleaf seedlots often have significant quantities of empty or partially filled seeds. Density-gravity tables offer the best option for removing empty seeds from large-sized seedlots. With smaller lots typically used in research projects, flotation in the chemical pentane is very effective (McLemore 1965).

In addition to longleaf seeds being large, they also have seedcoats that are fibrous and can carry significant populations of pathogenic fungi (Barnett and Pesacreta 1993, Pawuk 1978). Germination of less vigorous seeds may be improved by treating with a sterilant, such as hydrogen peroxide (Barnett 1976c), or applying a fungicidal drench that reduces *Fusarium* and *Pythium* populations (Barnett and Pesacreta 1993).

As technology for producing and handling longleaf pine seeds advanced, research on other pine species began so they could be handled equally well. In most situations, seeds of the other southern pines were more easily collected, processed, and stored than for longleaf pine.

Seed Storage and Testing

Storing longleaf pine seeds was a significant problem and subject to numerous studies. Early in the program, guidelines for successfully storing longleaf seeds were developed—drying to 8–10 percent moisture content and holding at subfreezing temperatures of 25 °F (-4 °C) or lower (Barnett 1969, Barnett and McLemore 1970, McLemore 1961c).

Longleaf pine seeds of good quality can be stored without significant losses in viability for at least 20 years, if held under the recommended conditions of low-seed moisture contents and storage temperatures (Barnett 1969, Barnett and Jones 1993). Other species can be held for longer periods. Slash and shortleaf *(P. echinata)* pine seeds have remained viable for up to 50 years when held under less than ideal conditions (Barnett and Vozzo 1985, Wakeley and Barnett 1968).

To evaluate if seeds stored for 7 years would perform well when direct seeded, Barnett (1964) conducted a series of studies and determined that stored seeds performed equally well as freshly collected seeds.

Testing is critical when using stored seeds. Although seeds can be tested at an organization's facility, the Eastern Tree Seed Laboratory at Dry Branch, GA, was established by the Forest Service in the early 1950s to provide this service. Now expanded to be the National Tree Seed Laboratory (NTSL), it provides for standardized and internationally recognized seed testing capability for forest tree and understory plant seeds. This service is particularly important as a third-party evaluation to meet the need for international sales and to resolve potential conflicts of interest.

Testing should be done soon after collecting and processing to determine initial seed quality. Also, seeds in storage should be tested periodically to determine if seeds are losing viability or vigor. Especially, stored seeds should be evaluated prior to use to establish appropriate sowing rates based on the quality of the seeds. The NTSL will provide these tests for a reasonable fee.

Storing Repellent-Treated Seeds

Seeding operations should be carefully scheduled to minimize time between seed treating and sowing. Sometimes delays are unavoidable, especially when seeds must be shipped or there are interruptions in time of sowing.

Seeds treated with repellents can be held for several weeks in a well-ventilated, unheated space or in a cold room at any temperature down to 0 °F (-18 °C). If seeds must be kept until the following year, they should be dried to 10 percent moisture content and stored between 0 °F (-18 °C) and 25 °F (-4 °C). The repellent coating will not lose its effectiveness even after 1 year of storage (Barnett and McLemore 1966, McLemore and Barnett 1966).

Stratification

In nature, longleaf pine seeds germinate in the fall soon after release from cones and are generally considered nondormant and do not require stratification or prechilling treatments (Mann 1970). However, some evaluations indicate an increase in speed of germination as a result of such treatment (Karrfalt 1988). Other studies show a potential reduction in total germination as a result of just 14 days of stratification (Barnett and Pesacreta 1993). So, stratification is not generally recommended for longleaf pine.

Other southern pine species exhibit some level of dormancy. Studies to determine the nature of dormancy in these seeds indicate that the proportion of the weight of the seed coat to total seed weight is closely related to level of dormancy (Barnett 1972). Seeds of loblolly pine are the most dormant of southern pine species and seeds from more northern and eastern sources exhibit the deepest dormancy (Barnett 1976b, 1991).

McLemore began a series of studies to develop recommendations for preparing loblolly pine seeds for sowing. Early evaluations indicated that a minimum of 30 days of stratification were needed to ensure prompt and complete germination when seeds are sown in the early spring (McLemore and Czabator 1961).

Aerated soaks are an approach to hastening germination of dormant seeds when time is lacking for lengthy stratification procedures. While not as effective as stratification, speed of germination can be significantly improved by using aerated soaks (Barnett 1971).

Information on the current knowledge on how to collect, process, treat, and store longleaf pine seeds has been summarized by Barnett and McGilvary (2002).

WHERE AND WHAT TO SEED

Where to Seed

Direct seeding was developed for use on forest lands that generally fall into two categories: (1) open lands, or (2) those partially or wholly occupied by brush and low-value hardwoods (Derr and Mann 1971).

Open areas typically have a grass sod cover, and these areas were often seeded with longleaf, loblolly, or slash pines. Such sites are relatively inexpensive to plant with bareroot seedlings, but seeding large acreages was faster and prompted many such operations. Seeding of longleaf pine, which is difficult to successfully plant with bareroot stock, was found to be an effective means of regenerating this species.

Direct seeding was also found to be useful in restocking stands destroyed by wildfire and wind storms. Salvage cutting of resulting dead timber typically scarifies the soil, creating an excellent seedbed.

In the 1950s, many pine sites were occupied by brush and hardwoods. Although such sites were ideal for reforestation, the low-value hardwoods needed to be destroyed by either mechanical or chemical treatments (Wheeler and Cassady 1956). Once the hardwoods were killed, the areas could be seeded without removal of the dead debris.

An industrial forester for T.L. James Company evaluating a cutover site for its potential for direct seeding.

Other sites where seeding was effectively used included mountainous soils that are often rocky, spoil banks left after strip mining, and heavy clay soils that are difficult to plant.

Some soil or terrain conditions are unsuitable for direct seeding or may require special treatment. These areas include tracts of deep upland sandy soils or areas in the extreme western portion of the pine range where the soil surface dries so rapidly that moisture is inadequate to sustain germination of broadcast-sown seed (Derr and Mann 1971). On such sites, the seeds must be covered with ½ to ¾ inch of soil to obtain germination and sustain seedling growth (Hodges and Scheer 1962, Jones 1963, Shipman 1963).

Sowing should not be attempted on poorly drained sites where seed or seedlings will be under water for more than 1 or 2 weeks (McReynolds 1960, Miller 1957).

In summary, sites suitable for seeding include most of those available for commercial pine production in the South. Among these sites are wide variations in soils and conditions. Usually, some site preparation is needed, but it may vary from intensive treatments that are essential for survival and growth to simple methods used primarily for increasing initial stocking levels (Derr and Mann 1971).

What Species to Seed

The need for regenerating large areas of cutover longleaf pine forests was the driving force for developing direct seeding technology. It is not surprising then that longleaf was the desired species for regenerating many sites across the South. However, lack of seed availability limited its use for years. Some landowners, too, preferred using other species because of the slow initiation of height growth of longleaf pine.

Loblolly pine, then, became widely used in seeding operations in the upper Coastal Plain (Mann and Derr 1961), and slash pine was generally used in the coastal flatwoods (Mann and Derr 1964). Wells (1969) and Shoulders and Tiarks (1980) did much to establish guidelines for species selection on specific soil types.

Basic direct-seeding procedures do not vary greatly from species to species. The same repellent formulation can be used and sowing methods are essentially alike. There are, however, species differences in fruiting habits, seed size, seed dormancy, and site requirements that affect sowing procedures. These and other relevant species characteristics that affect seeding are discussed by Derr and Mann (1971).

SITES AND SEEDBED PREPARATION

Selecting sites to be seeded to pines and choosing presowing treatments are closely related tasks. Methods vary in cost and intensity, but in most cases conditions on the site determine the methods to be used.

Site preparation for direct seeding has two objectives: (1) to expose the mineral soil that seeds need for germination, and (2) to control competing vegetation that will interfere with the survival and growth of the new stands (Boggs and Wittwer 1993, Derr and Mann 1971).

Fire is the simplest and least expensive method of site preparation, and on open sites it is often sufficient. On areas with hardwood brush and trees, it typically is combined with mechanical or chemical treatments. Whatever means are chosen, fairly complete removal of competing hardwood trees is usually needed and the likelihood of sprout growth must be considered. To control trees large enough to be treated individually, chemical application methods, such as tree injectors and basal sprays, were developed (Peevy 1960, 1961). Dense stands of small stems were usually eliminated by mechanical treatments or in some instances by chemical spraying treatments (Peevy and Burns 1959).

Prescribed Fire

Prescribed or controlled burns are an option on most sites and may be the only treatment needed for open, grassy sites. The light grass rough that develops several months after the fire provides a better germination environment for longleaf pine than does newly burned sites (Derr and Mann 1959).

Successful seeding of loblolly pine on a mine spoil bank in north Alabama.

Exposure of mineral soil is a desired effect from a presowing burn, but for longleaf pine there are additional benefits. For example, fire removes foliage infected with brown-spot needle disease, which can develop on sites where grass-stage seedlings from previous stands exist. A single burn will reduce competition, but will not provide sufficient control of small hardwoods and brush. Sprouting regrowth is often rapid and may require additional treatment.

Disking

Disking became a more intensive treatment for seeding open, grassy sites and where palmetto (*Sabal adans*) and gallberry (*Ilex coriacea*) were abundant. In such open sites, disking confined to strips, separated by 6- to 7-foot undisked areas, was a very effective treatment.

Several studies with longleaf, slash, and loblolly pine demonstrated that disking markedly improved survival in dry years (Derr and Mann 1971, Lohrey 1974). Early seedling growth of loblolly and slash pine was also improved by disking. After 10 years, however, this initial growth advantage was lost (Haywood 1983).

Disking elevated seed beds, or mounding, became a common practice on flatwood sites where water tables are high. Seeding on these areas resulted in improved seedling survival and early height growth as a result of removal of competing vegetation (Russell and Rhame 1961), but frequently there was no long-term benefit (Mann and Derr 1970).

Simple broadcast sowing is effective on disked ground, but more cost-effective treatments can be achieved with machines that drop seeds in rows and have packing wheels that put them into firm contact with the soil.

Amelioration

Direct seeding techniques were extended to sites that required modification for optimum growth of pines. These treatments, sometimes referred to as site amelioration, include drainage, high bedding, and creation of artificial tussocks. These were developed to improve seeding performance in low coastal areas and other places where drainage is slow and water tables are high during much of the year (Jarvis and Beers 1965).

Drainage was shown to result in a striking growth response on water-logged sites. High bedding, or mounding, is an intensive disking treatment done with equipment that elevates the seedbed by 5 or 6 inches.

Top: Prescribed burning became a primary practice for reducing vegetative competition prior to seeding. **Bottom:** *Row seeding with a tractor-drawn disk seeder and packing wheel developed by the T.L. James Company.*

12

Bedding became a popular method of removing excess water from the rooting zone and improving soil aeration. Growth response to bedding was found to vary significantly (Derr and Mann 1977, Mann and Derr 1970), largely because of differences in the amount of well-aerated soil bedding provides during the wet winter period (McKee and Shoulders 1970, 1974).

For 8-year-old slash pine, beds that raised the rooting zone 18 inches or more above the water table during January and February were effective in promoting tree growth, whereas beds that raised the soil <18 inches resulted in less aboveground biomass (Shoulders and McKee 1973).

Site preparation treatments, such as disking and mounding, typically improve seeding and planting success and early growth primarily by reducing competition from herbaceous vegetation (Tiarks and Haywood 1981).

Control of Competing Vegetation

Even before the development of direct seeding, the need for chemical treatments for controlling undesired, low-grade hardwoods became a research focus (Cassady and Mann 1954). Much of the forest land in the West Gulf region not completely devoid of trees was covered with non-merchantable scrub hardwoods, and removal of this material was critical for restoring productive pine forests.

Fred A. Peevy, first employee of the ARC in 1946, was responsible for developing chemical control techniques for these low-quality trees—primarily blackjack oak (*Quercus marilandica*), post oak (*Q. stellata*), red oak (*Q. falcata*), sweetgum (*Liquidamber styraciflua*), and hickory (*Carya* spp.).

Ammate® was an early chemical that Peevy (1947) developed methodologies for use in forestry. Soon, Ammate® was replaced by the agricultural chemicals 2,4-D® and 2,4,5T®. These became the mainstay forestry treatments for a number of years (Peevy 1960, 1961). As environmental problems became evident with these chemicals, Peevy began to evaluate a number of newer and safer products and developed recommendations for using them for control of a range of upland hardwood species.

Peevy's pioneering research was applied quickly into the direct seeding programs. Seeding of sites converted from low-quality hardwoods was accomplished by sowing seeds as the hardwoods were killed by chemical treatments. Use of direct seeding was a particularly effective method of converting these sites to pines because the deadened standing hardwood timber did not have to be removed.

Top: High bedding or mounding became a common practice to prepare wet sites for seeding or planting. ***Bottom:*** *Fred A. Peevy applying a chemical basal spray to a blackjack oak.*

TIMING AND SOWING RATES

There are two distinct sowing seasons—spring and fall. Fall sowing is generally recommended for longleaf pine. Seeds of the other major southern pines that exhibit some dormancy—loblolly, slash, and shortleaf—are best sown in the spring after stratification.

The best time for fall sowing of longleaf pine is at an early date after natural seedfall when the soil has been recharged by 2 to 4 inches of rain (Derr and Mann 1971). If rains are delayed, longleaf can be sown well into December. Longleaf will germinate throughout winter, but cold weather slows the process and lowers seedling yields.

For species sown in the spring, timing is defined as the transition period between winter dormancy and appearance of new foliage—about the time first blooms appear on red bud (*Cercis canadensis*) and red maple (*Acer rubrum*) trees (Derr and Mann 1971). Stratified seeds sown in mid-February usually complete germination by mid-April. Delays in sowing may adversely affect results (Hatchell 1966).

Sowing rates vary considerably, even within a species, by quality of the seeds, method of sowing, and stocking desired by the landowner.

General recommendations for broadcast seeding are about 3 pounds of seed per acre for longleaf pine, 1 pound for slash and loblolly, and 0.5 pound for shortleaf (table 1). These provide rates between 12,000 and 20,000 viable seeds per acre and result in initial stands ranging between 2,000 and 5,000 seedlings per acre. For sowing rows or spots, the rates should be much less (table 1).

A difficulty in broadcast seeding is the frequent overstocking of the resulting stands. The stocking levels vary considerably by environmental conditions and degree of site preparation, as well as seed quality and preconditioning. If there is experience in seeding similar areas to those proposed, the sowing rate may be adjusted downward. The frequent need for precommercial thinning resulted in techniques developed to reduce overstocking by sowing disked strips, rows, and for small landowners, spots (Lohrey 1970, Mann and Burns 1965).

SEED DISTRIBUTION

Sowing pine seeds can be accomplished by a number of methods depending on the size of the area to be seeded and the availability of specialized sowing equipment. Seeds of different species vary considerably in flow characteristics through seeding equipment. The shape of pine seeds affect flow and dewinged longleaf seeds are particularly difficult due to the adherence of the wing to the seed coat; it is broken off during processing, and a wing stub results. In an attempt to improve the flow, aluminum flakes were added to the repellent seed treatment (Derr 1964).

Pelleting of pine seeds was evaluated in an attempt to improve flow characteristics for use in seeding equipment. The results of these trials indicated that the pelleting material had an adverse effect on germination due to the amount of material needed to obtain round pelleted seeds and the epigeal nature of pine seed germination (the germinating seed is raised by the root radicle growing into the soil).

Table 1—Average number of seeds per pound and suggested sowing rates per acre

Species	Seeds per pound[a]	Weight of dry seeds per acre for seeding					
		Broadcast		Rows[b]		Spots[c]	
		No.	Lbs.	No.	Lbs.	No.	Lbs.
Longleaf pine	4,700	15,000	3.24	2,900	0.63	4,350	0.94
Slash pine	14,500	14,000	1.11	2,900	0.23	4,350	0.35
Loblolly pine	18,400	12,000	0.75	2,150	0.14	3,650	0.23
Shortleaf pine	48,000	20,000	0.48	4,350	0.10	5,800	0.14

[a]Dry untreated seed with viability of 95 to 100 percent: averages from Wakeley (1954)

[b]Rows 10 feet apart for all species. Spacing within rows: 15 feet for longleaf and slash, 20 feet for loblolly and 10 feet for shortleaf

[c]Spots spaced 6 x 10 feet. 6 seeds per spot for longleaf and slash, 5 per spot for loblolly and 8 per spot for shortleaf

Source: Campbell (1982b)

Longleaf pine seed showing epigeal type of germination.

Ground Methods

Hand sowing—This is the oldest form of direct seeding. But, as seeding technology improved and areas to be seeded increased, mechanized ground-sowing equipment was developed. The simplest of such equipment are hand-operated cyclone seeders. These can be very efficient for seeding small areas.

Hand-cranked seeders have a simple metering device and have an effective swath of about 16 feet. Daily production of about 15 acres per individual is common (Derr and Mann 1971). Organization of crews is straightforward and flexible; crew members walking about 16 feet apart can effectively seed sites up to 100 acres in size.

Another hand-sowing technique for small acreages is spot sowing. It was developed specifically for small landowners where vehicle operation and other seedbed treatments such as fire are impractical. A spot is raked, hoed, or kicked free of vegetation and litter, and 5 to 8 seeds are dropped and pressed into mineral soil with the foot (Lohrey and Jones 1983). Several hand tools have been developed to facilitate the task (Burns 1961, Mann 1962).

Spot seeding is better adapted to areas with a ground cover of hardwood litter than sites with a grass sod. Prepared sites should be at least 1 foot in diameter and the cleared material scattered to prevent blowback onto the site. At the recommended rate of 1,000 spots per acre, 2 to 4 acres can be seeded per man-day (Campbell 1982a).

Tractor seeding—While hand seeding is possible on small areas, most ground seeding has been done with row-seeding machines. Many types of row seeders have been developed. Some simply drop seeds on previously prepared ground, but many plow a furrow or disk a narrow strip and meter out seeds and press them into mineral soil with packing wheels. Many of these types of seeders are described by Derr and Mann (1971).

Disk seeders have two main drawbacks. First, they leave rough beds on which considerable soil is lost by silting. Second, disking in cool, wet weather fails to control grass adequately (Derr and Mann 1971).

This seeding equipment typically uses modified agricultural seed-dispensing devices that are inaccurate on rough forest sites. A seeder that employs a vacuum system to move seeds from a hopper and drop them at precise intervals was developed to improve seed distribution (Richardson 1965).

Aerial Methods

About 75 percent of the total acreage seeded has been from the air, either with small fixed wing aircraft or helicopters (Derr and Mann 1971). On operations exceeding 500 acres,

Preparing a spot for hand seeding with the use of a fire rake.

15

Thomas C. Croker demonstrating a row seeder which elevates a low ridge in a plowed furrow and drops seeds that will be pressed into the soil.

Effectiveness of seeding differs little whether applied by planes or helicopters. Both types require constant checking of equipment and precision flying for best results. The main distinction between the two types of aircraft is in the width of the flight strip; helicopters can seed a strip 100 feet wide, while small planes are limited to about 65 feet wide. The primary advantage of helicopters is in the time for loading seeds; helicopters can land on or near the site, while planes usually operate from a landing strip miles away.

Accurate aerial seeding requires good ground control, which is often difficult on rolling topography or where there is a canopy of hardwoods. Preparation needed in most cases includes a large-scale map of the area to be seeded, location of the flagman's position for each flight line, and marking of tract boundaries. Detailed discussion of the development of the field layout for aerial seeding is provided by Derr and Mann (1971).

Calibrating Seeding Equipment

Proper calibration—adjustment of the seed release mechanism to the desired sowing rate—is important in all operations. For best results the rate of seed flow should be checked frequently during the seeding operation and adjusted as necessary.

aerial seeding is comparable to the cost of most ground methods of broadcast seeding. It is fast and frequently the only practical means of sowing inaccessible terrain or debris-covered areas. When properly calibrated, aerial seeding is an accurate seeding method, giving complete coverage regardless of topography, brush, or debris.

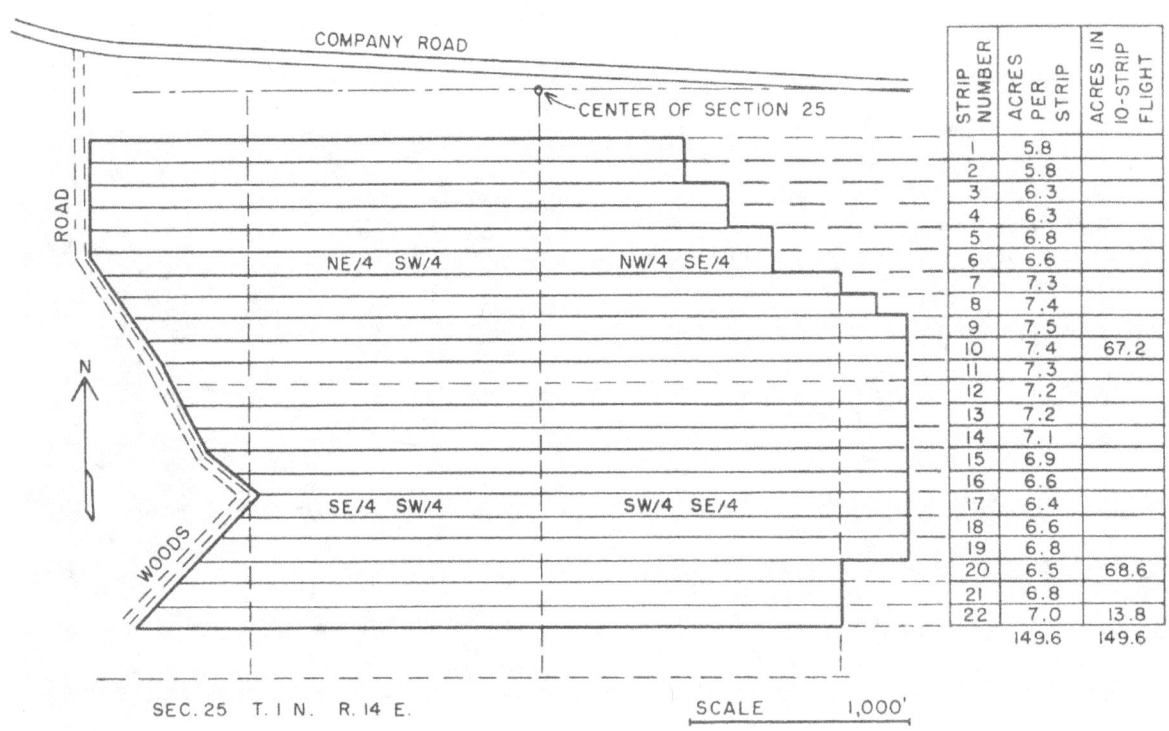

An example map of a site to be aerially seeded showing flight lines and acreages for each. Source: Derr and Mann (1971).

16

Calibration procedures for both ground and aerial equipment are described in depth by Derr and Mann (1971). Readers are referred to this publication for specific details.

APPRAISALS

Seed losses begin on the day of seeding and continue throughout the germination period. Once germination occurs, attrition of the resulting seedlings begins. A successful seeding is one where losses are minimized so that adequate first-year stocking is achieved using the least amount of seeds. The landowner must have a reliable estimate of controllable losses, achievable stand density, and losses from uncontrollable factors such as drought.

Two or three estimates are normally needed during the establishment period. They are to determine predator activity, initial stocking, and stocking at the end of the first year. Direct seeding often has been done without adequate appraisals, and well-stocked stands have been "discovered" several years after a cursory examination categorized them as failures. Even worse, perhaps, are those stands carried on the record as stocked when they initially failed.

Estimating Predator Activity

Finding the cause of failures of seeding is often a difficult task. Although birds have been the principal problem in southern pine seeding, other biological agents will cause problems in certain areas. Observation stations, where repeated examinations can be made, are essential for evaluating predator activity and determining cause(s) of failures in seeding trials.

An effective observation station consists of an identification stake and two small, cleared spots containing 25 treated seeds each located near the stake. An additional screened spot with at least 10 seeds is usually added to provide an estimate of field germination (Derr and Mann 1971).

The number of stations needed varies with the acreage of the seeding and variety of cover conditions. Fifty well-dispersed stations are usually adequate for areas of 500 to 1,000 acres in size. More may be needed on larger areas or where there are wide differences in site or cover conditions. For small areas, the number can be scaled down, but 15 are about the minimum needed to achieve meaningful data.

Frequency of examination of the stations may range from daily to weekly. The number of seeds destroyed or missing should be recorded and notes taken on evidence left by predators. Germinated seeds should be marked with pins because seedlings are often destroyed with little evidence of cause.

Observation stations simply provide a quick means of detecting damage. When damage does occur, further checking is needed to determine the nature of the losses and to evaluate the seed treatments. If rodents seem to be a significant problem and only thiram was used as the

Aerial seeding being used with a fixed-wing plane with seed distribution controlled by a flagman on the ground.

Observation station with center stake, two spots with 25 treated seeds each, and a screened spot with 10 seeds to evaluate germination potential.

17

repellent, the addition of the rodent repellent capsicum into the formulation may be needed to achieve better seeding success (Nolte and Barnett 2000).

Identifying Causes of Seed and Seedling Losses

Despite the general effectiveness of repellent coatings, local losses due to various agents will occur. Checking of the observation stations at least weekly during the progress of germination will provide information on the number of intact seeds and hulled seeds, type of damage to the seed and seedlings, insect activity, and condition of the repellent coating. Marking germinated seeds with small pins provides a method of detecting losses that occur during advanced stages of germination.

Typically, birds consume seeds either by swallowing them whole or by shattering the seed coat and removing the endosperm. So, sometimes no remnants are left for potential identification of the predator.

However, many predators leave characteristic seed hull and fragments behind. Some rodents carry seeds a few yards to a protective cover and leave a neat pile of seed hulls where they have been feeding. Derr and Mann (1959) provide descriptive damage to seed remains that are caused by a number of predators. This information is helpful in determining local seed predators.

Loss of established seedlings immediately after germination is a problem, particularly with fall-sown longleaf pine seeds. Clipping of the germinated seedlings is the most frequent type of damage. These seedlings provide green and succulent vegetation at a time in the year when there is little green-plant material available to sustain small animals. Rabbits are a frequent cause of this type of clipping. If rabbit populations are known to be large, seeding winter grass near the seeded area may draw rabbits from the seeded area and limit the extent of the damage.

Although losses from predators typically occur following seeding operations, climatic conditions or poor seed quality may also be responsible for some failures. It is important, then, to install observation stations, or plots, to detect any unusual damage to seeds and seedlings.

Seedling Inventories

Survival of established seedlings during the first year is critical for all southern pines. Mortality may vary greatly by climate, soil type, and cover conditions. Summer droughts are a frequent problem throughout the South.

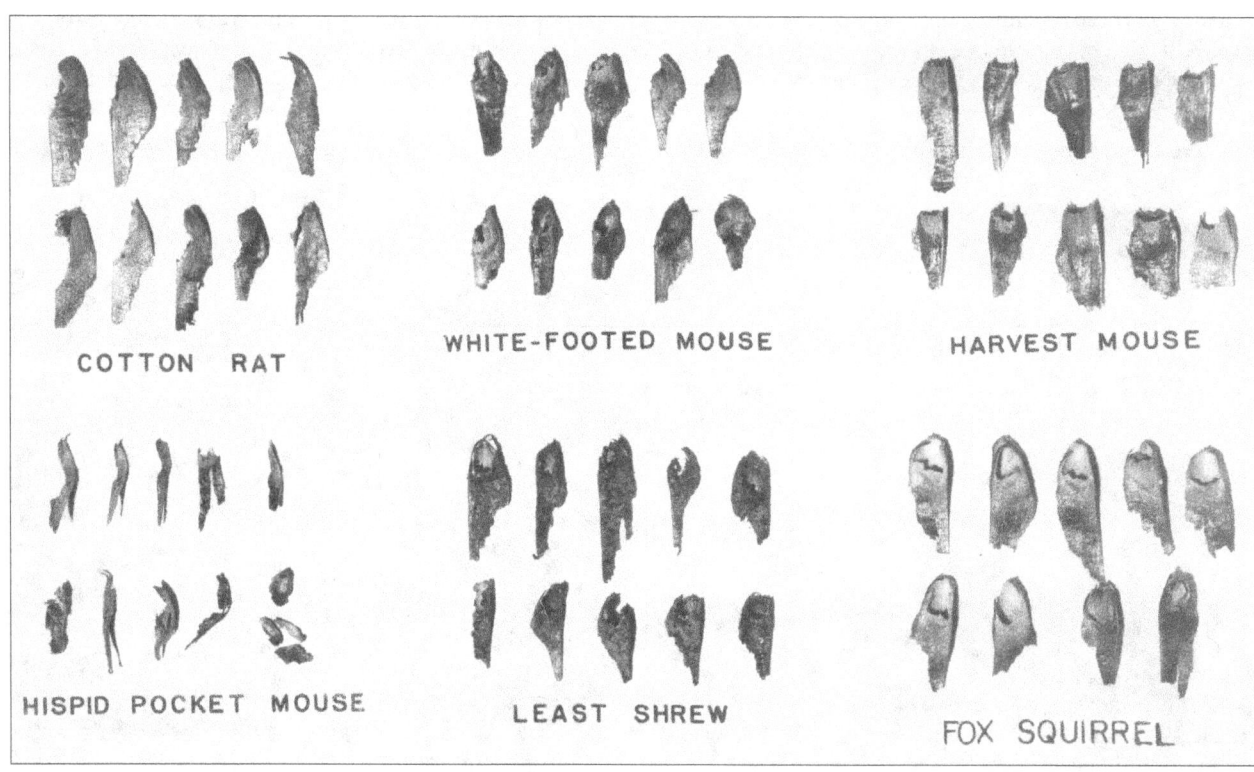

Characteristic damage to untreated longleaf seeds by seed predators in central Louisiana. These hull fragments were obtained from caged predators. (Photo by Brooke Meanley, U.S. Fish and Wildlife Service)

18

Seedling inventories are needed to determine seeding success. H.J. Derr and B.F. McLemore, above, are filmed making an inventory for an early 1960s Forest Service movie on direct seeding.

To establish causes of early seedling losses, two seedling inventories are generally advised—one at the beginning of the summer when germination is completed, the other at the end of the first growing season when mortality from summer drought is past. The earlier inventory indicates the efficiency of the repellents. The second provides an estimate of overall seeding success. If drought or other adverse conditions occur during the second or third year, additional investigations may be important in determining long-term success of seeding operations.

Seeding success of broadcast-seeded areas can be determined by estimating the number of seedlings per acre and the distribution of these seedlings—these two values are closely related. Tree percent, the ratio of seedlings to seed, is often calculated. It should be about 25 percent in early summer (that is, 1 seedling for 4 seeds); if it is lower than this something unusual likely occurred.

Stocking, a measure of seedling distribution, is normally expressed as the percentage of milacre (1/1,000 acre) sample plots that have one or more seedlings. Land managers judge success frequently by the stocking percent after the first growing season. Usually a minimum stocking percentage of 55 is needed as a judgment of success (Derr and Mann 1971). Adequate distribution is rarely obtained with less than 750 seedlings per acre.

Number of seedlings per acre and stocking can be determined by installation of sampling plots. Circular

milacre plots with a radius of 44.7 inches are ideal for sampling broadcast seedlings as only a sweep of the plot radius using a stiff wire or stick from a central point is needed to establish plot boundaries. Twenty-five is the minimum number of plots for any seeded area. On large areas, one plot per acre has been used successfully (Ezell 2012).

Appraisals of seedling success on broadcast-sown disked strips, and row- and spot-seeding require modification of the evaluation techniques. These modifications are described in detail by Derr and Mann (1971).

STAND PROTECTION AND MANAGEMENT

After the first growing season, mortality from drought usually is not a major problem and aggressive height growth begins for most southern pine species. Seedlings usually outgrow competing vegetation and the primary cause of mortality is fire. So, protection from wildfire for the first few years is necessary for most southern pine species.

Use of Prescribed Fire

Unlike most southern pine species, longleaf pine seedlings do not immediately begin height growth and may remain in a grass stage for several years unless the stands are properly managed. While in the grass stage, a number of problems may contribute to slow initiation of height growth. Unless site preparation treatments are effective enough to delay growth of competing vegetation, prescribed fire may be needed to release longleaf seedlings from overtopping vegetation and reduce amounts of diseased foliage resulting from brown-spot needle blight. Longleaf seedlings tolerate fire during the grass stage, and burning results in increased availability to light that stimulates seedling growth. Such use of prescribed fire usually takes place in the second or third year following seeding.

Seedling infection with brown-spot disease was a significant problem when direct seeding was being developed. Stands of old-growth longleaf pines may have occurred many years earlier, but longleaf seedlings in the grass stage persisted on many of these sites. These seedlings were typically infected with brown-spot needle blight and provided a source for the disease spores to be sustained and to infect newly seeded or planted longleaf pines.

There was, then, the need for the use of prescribed fire to burn the disease-infected foliage and present an opportunity for seedling growth to occur before the infection again became severe enough to limit growth. However, if a site does not have longleaf seedlings in the grass stage

Longleaf pine seedlings following a prescribed burn to reduce competition and brown-spot infected foliage.

and seeded trees begin height growth promptly, brown-spot needle disease will not be a major problem. Limited populations of brown-spot spores occur on land not previously occupied by longleaf pine.

Even if brown-spot disease is not a problem, use of fire is an important aspect of longleaf pine management. Prescribed burning studies were originally installed to evaluate ways to improve forage production and quality (Barnett and others 2011). But in these studies, Grelen (1975, 1983) established that burning of longleaf pine stands in May was more effective than in the dormant winter season for controlling

competing woody vegetation. This schedule of burning increased survival and growth of longleaf pine seedlings. These findings that prescribed burning in the spring increases longleaf performance has become an important aspect of longleaf pine management.

Precommercial Thinning

One of the problems facing landowners seeding their land has been overstocking of trees that frequently require precommercial thinning. Seeding rates were developed in anticipation of losses of seeds to predators and reduced germination affected by less than ideal weather conditions. Also, mortality of seedlings to drought and other adverse factors are expected during the first year after seeding. When conditions following seeding are more favorable than anticipated, numbers of seedlings per acre at the end of the first year may reach 5,000 or more.

Maintaining low stand densities can increase diameter growth, reduce rotations, shorten times to first thinning, and lesson potential fire mortality. High levels of stocking may negate these positive effects. Numerous studies were installed to address the overstocking problem that sometimes results from direct seeding.

Slash and loblolly pine stands were established by direct seeding with the intent of obtaining high stocking levels (Lohrey 1972, 1973b). These studies resulted in over 5,000 seedlings per acre. When the stands were 3 years old, precommercial thinning—consisting of both selective

Unthinned 11-year-old slash pine with initial stocking of 5,000 stems per acre.

Eleven-year-old slash pine thinned by hand to 750 stems per acre at age 3 years.

hand and mechanical treatments—were installed. When the stands were 11 years old, results from the thinning treatments were evaluated.

These and other studies indicate that stands with levels of stocking of over 2,000 per acre should be precommercially thinned. To minimize costs, stands should be thinned when they are 3 or 4 years old. Reducing stocking to 500 and 750 stems per acre will result in optimum diameter growth without reducing volume production. Thinning by cutting swaths mechanically was found as effective as selecting individual stems to be cut. Removing swaths about 10 to 12 feet wide will provide access for protection and stand management. Thinning can be done with rotary mowers or rolling drum choppers (Lohrey 1977, Mann and Lohrey 1974), or by chemical treatments (Williams and others 2008). If thinned with mechanical equipment, operations carried out in late summer are more effective in limiting sprouting of cut shortleaf, slash, and loblolly pine seedlings than operations earlier in the year (Campbell 1985b).

An analysis of the economics of precommercial thinning shows that it is a financially attractive investment (Fox and others 1976, Williams and others 2008). Stands in excess of 2,000 seedlings per acre should receive precommercial thinning with the goal to reduce the number of seedlings down to 400 to 800 trees per acre. Thinning can be most easily done at the age 3 or 4 years, but additional gains in tree growth can be achieved by treatments applied as late as age 10.

ADVANTAGES OF DIRECT SEEDING

Direct seeding can be an effective practice for regenerating the southern pines. On many sites, direct seeding may be more economical than planting nursery-grown seedlings or waiting for natural regeneration. Seeding may be the best choice on sites where access, terrain, or drainage conditions make planting difficult, although the process requires considerable technical skill and knowledge.

The choice of seeding depends on the landowner's goals and economic situation, as well as the condition of the site and the capability of the land manager. Advantages of direct seeding are discussed further.

Lower Initial Cost

The most notable advantage of direct seeding is lower initial cost when compared to planting nursery stock (Ezell 2012). The cost of seeding is usually less than one-half that of the cost of planting seedlings. The reasons for the reduced costs are: seeds are usually less expensive than seedlings; labor, equipment, and facility costs are lower; and site preparation costs are normally less expensive.

It is important to remember that these cost savings are for the initial seedling establishment. Because of the lower costs, however, seeding should be an attractive alternative for small private landowners.

Flexibility

Another advantage is that direct seeding is easier to accomplish in remote or inaccessible areas. Although much of the Coastal Plain in the South is accessible, seeding has advantages in mountainous areas with rocky soils.

Top: Precommercial thinning of a young loblolly pine stand by rotary mower mounted on a farm tractor. ***Bottom:*** *Seeded longleaf seedlings are beginning height growth on a previously harvested longleaf pine site.*

Seeding allows landowners to quickly respond to large areas affected by wildfires or other natural disasters. Seeds from storage can be retrieved, treated, and sown within relatively short periods, whereas, nursery stock may require a year or more before large quantities of seedlings are available for planting.

Direct seeding, as does planting, provides an opportunity to change the species or genetic composition of a forest area. This is important where forests have been highly degraded. It presents an option to restore a desired pine species to land on which high-quality forests previously flourished.

Hard to Plant Species and Low-Quality Sites

Some species, notably longleaf pine, are difficult to regenerate by planting of bareroot nursery stock. These problems were the primary reason for the initial development of direct seeding.

Direct seeding is also a good alternative for regenerating low-quality sites. Cost of planting such sites may bring into question the economy of planting such areas. So, lower initial seeding costs provide a good opportunity for regenerating sites of low productivity.

Natural Root Systems

The root systems of trees that develop from direct seeding are considered natural. Planted seedlings may have distorted roots that end up in an "L-shape" or "J-shape" if the planting hole is not deep enough. As much as 30 percent of planted shortleaf pine in Arkansas lacked a taproot compared to only 15 percent of seeded seedlings (Harrington and others 1986). A distorted root system may reduce growth, and shallow planting does reduce the survival of planted stock (Brissette and Barnett 1989).

DISADVANTAGES OF DIRECT SEEDING

The use of direct seeding has declined from its widespread use in the 1960s and 1970s. There are a number of reasons for this situation. Disadvantages of seeding are discussed in the following sections.

Poor Control of Spacing and Stocking

One of the most notable problems with direct seeding is poor control of tree spacing and stocking (number of trees per acre). The number of seeds sown is based on assumption of acceptable rates of survival. If environmental conditions are ideal, it is possible that too many trees will survive, resulting in an overstocked situation that will require

precommercial thinning to correct. Maintaining stands with over 2,000 seedlings per acre will result in reduced growth and financial return (Williams and others 2008). The opposite situation is also frequent; establishment may not be adequate to fully stock the area. This situation is even more costly to the landowner because additional site preparation and planting may be needed.

High Mortality on Droughty Soils

Another disadvantage of seeding is high mortality on droughty soils. During the first month after germination, the root system is still near the soil surface (Ezell 2012). If the landowner needs to maximize profits, seeding may result in poor stocking and be less desirable than planting in areas with droughty soils.

Seeded stands do, however, provide attractive yields and profits to landowners. Seeded loblolly pine stands at age 22 yielded only slightly lower yields than adjacent planted stands (Campbell 1975).

Limited Use of Genetically Improved Seed Sources

Seeding normally does not take advantage of the opportunity to use seeds from genetically improved sources due to less availability and higher cost. In recent years genetically improved material of some species is available. However, these seeds are still generally more expensive and large quantities are needed, especially for broadcast

Longleaf pine seed with dewinged seed coats—seed coat wing stubs remain. Genetically improved seeds have seldom been used for direct seeding.

seeding where tree percent (ratio of seeds sown to seedlings obtained) is significantly less than for planting.

Limited Availability of Large, Open Sites

Seeding is best suited for use on large, open tracts of forest land. Such open areas are now seldom available. This is one of the major reasons for the decline in use of direct seeding. Planting offers better control of spacing and stocking than seeding on highly productive forest land.

Less Effective Repellent Seed Coating

The removal of the rodent repellent, endrin, from the market reduced the efficacy of seeding on areas where rodents are major seed predators. Although no replacement chemical as effective as endrin has been found, capsicum—in combination with thiram—has been shown recently to significantly reduce rodent damage to seeds (Barnett 1998, Nolte and Barnett 2000). So, these repellents result in direct seeding remaining a viable option for reforestation.

Limited Availability of Personnel

An additional problem limiting successful application of seeding is the availability of specialists with a high degree of technical skill, knowledge, and experience with seeding (Williston and others 1998).

ROLE OF SEEDING IN THE REFORESTATION OF THE SOUTH

In the late 1940s and early 1950s, foresters in the South faced a huge reforestation problem—millions of acres of forest land clearcut in the early 1900s remained desolate and non-productive. Much of this land was previously occupied by mature stands of longleaf pines; however, the harvest was so complete that no seed source remained to allow for natural reproduction. Planting of longleaf pine was unreliable at that time.

The potential of direct seeding longleaf pine was especially appealing, and seeding studies began in the early 1950s. These evaluations determined that failures of seeding were primarily caused by bird and rodent predation. Key to the success of seeding was the development of repellents to limit predation. Finding effective repellents led to the need for supporting research programs that provided necessary seed production capacity, methods of eliminating competing undesired and low-quality hardwoods, and clarification of site-preparation needs. These supporting research programs were critical for

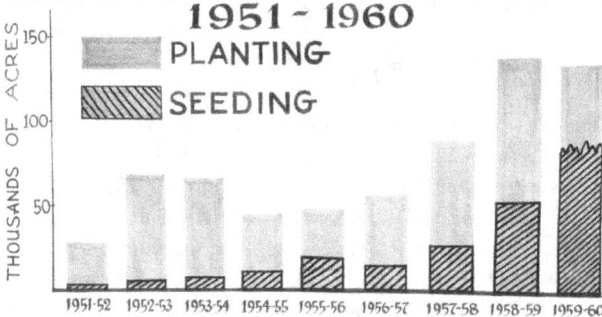

Growth of direct seeding in Louisiana as seeding technology developed. The chart was developed in 1960 to illustrate the expansion of direct seeding within Louisiana.

the implementation of large-scale seeding operations (Mann 1968, 1969; Mann and Burkhalter 1961).

The largest application of seeding remained in the West Gulf Coast region due to the huge areas of open land needing to be reforested and seeding was found to be well suited to such areas. However, seeding technology was quickly adapted and applied to meet reforestation needs throughout the United States and other locations across the World where coniferous species are grown (Mann 1965, Rietveld and Heidmann 1976, Vietmeyer 1981, Walters and Whitesell 1971).

Extent of Seeding Southern Pines

Although direct seeding was initially developed for reforesting longleaf pine, seeding technology was rapidly adapted to other southern pine species. Because of the rapidity in which reforestation could be achieved, the use of seeding quickly spread across the South.

Direct seeding was never meant to replace planting as a regeneration tool, but it was used over a 25-year period to aggressively reforest over 1,725,000 acres of forest land in the South (Campbell 1982b). Its greatest use has been in regenerating vast acreages of cutover forests that remained without a seed source needed for natural regeneration. Forest industry and public land managers quickly accepted and applied the technology to restore these deforested lands to productive use (Mann 1968, Mann and Burkhalter 1961).

Seeding was largely applied to reforest open areas of clearcut forests; however, many landowners began to see it as an inexpensive tool for reforesting small tracts (Campbell 1981b, Mann and Burns 1965). Currently, direct seeding is seen as a viable option for restoring sites of small land ownerships, and guidelines for the technology for this use are readily available (Duryea 1992, Ezell 2012, Gwaze and others 2005, Williston and others 1998).

Evaluation of Seeded Stands

The growth of direct seeded pines has been evaluated in a number of studies. At age 9, planted loblolly and slash pines were taller than seeded pines (Lohrey 1973a). For both species, the height difference was equivalent to about 1 year's growth. When the 1-year age difference between planted and seeded trees is considered, most of the seeding treatments compare favorably with planting.

Evaluations of the site preparation treatments showed that mechanical site-preparation treatments for direct seeding were generally not effective in boosting growth (Campbell 1981c). The treatments included planting, broadcast and swath seeding on a burned rough and on disked and mounded strips, and furrow seeding. Results showed that disking and furrowing enhanced first-year survival in a dry year, and mounding promoted growth on excessively wet sites. The early positive response to mechanical treatments seemed to result primarily from reduction in vegetative competition.

When growth of the Lohrey (1973a) study was measured at age 20 years (Campbell 1985a), planted loblolly pine yielded volumes that were not significantly higher than volumes on 3 of the 6 direct-seeding treatments. However, planted trees were fewer in number, larger in diameter, and more uniformly spaced than seeded trees. Slash

pine volumes were not significantly different by regeneration method.

In an effort to evaluate if growth projections of slash pine planted and seeded stands differed markedly, Lohrey (1984) developed equations for estimating total green or dry weight of stems or crowns and the ratio of merchantable stem to total stem weight. There were significant differences based on the size of trees that reflected development in response to variable tree spacing and 1-year difference in initial height.

In a more recent study, Haywood and Barnett (1994) found that 15 years after planting bareroot and container seedlings and seeding loblolly and slash pines in a comparative study that growth of seeded seedlings was slightly less than that of planted stock. This primarily reflects the age advantage of planted seedlings. The results do show that direct seeding can be a viable regeneration alternative, especially when regeneration costs are a limiting factor.

Lohrey (1987) developed site index curves for direct-seeded slash pine in Louisiana. The models that resulted were close to the existing ones for natural regenerated slash pine. In an expansion of this effort, site index curves for direct-seeded loblolly and longleaf pines were prepared (Cao and others 1997). These site index models provide short-term height projections for direct-seeded pines of these species in the mid-South.

CURRENT APPLICATION OF DIRECT SEEDING TECHNOLOGY

Today, use of direct seeding is limited. Traditional forest regeneration by natural seeding or planting of genetically improved nursery stock is the prevalent means of reforestation on highly productive sites.

Where Should Direct Seeding Be Used?

Basically, any site that can be planted with seedlings can be direct seeded. The primary exceptions are excessively droughty areas previously discussed. However, there are four areas where seeding has the greatest current application: (1) large areas requiring reforestation resulting from wildfires or other natural disasters, (2) remote or inaccessible areas, (3) low-productive sites where growth of trees would not make the cost of planting operations economically feasible, and (4) any area where a minimal investment is absolutely essential (Ezell 2012). The last category is important because many small private landowners cannot afford the cost of intensive site preparation and planting. It is better to direct seed these

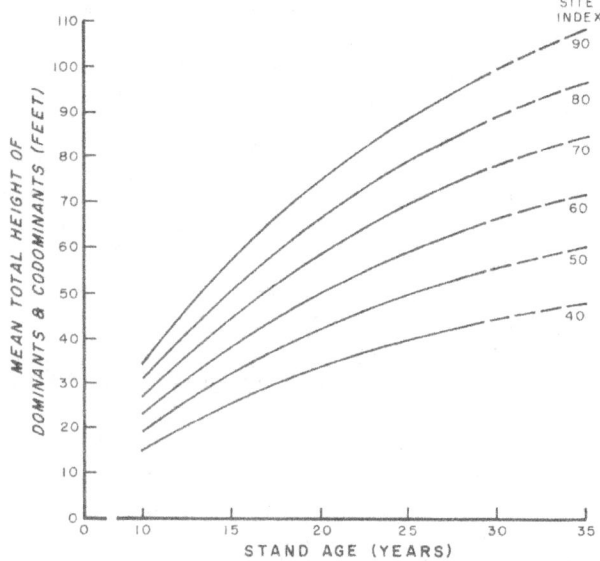

Site index curves, base age 25 years, for slash pine stands established by direct seeding. Source: Lohrey (1987)

areas rather than to allow them to grow up with undesirable species and brush.

What Species Are Best Suited For Direct Seeding?

Problems with the regeneration of longleaf pine were a primary reason for the development of direct seeding, and seeding remains an option for its regeneration. However, the development of container planting of longleaf is now a reliable and preferred method for its reforestation (Barnett and McGilvray 1997). Container seedlings are costly, but cost-share programs will lower the expense to the landowner.

Species selection will be affected by goals of ownership, but putting a species on the sites where it grows best and with less danger of loss results in the most successful direct seeding. Also, seed availability and treatments must be considered.

Sand pine (*P. clausa*) is a species ideally suited for direct seeding. It occurs on sandy, infertile soils in the Florida sandhills where low tree quality and productivity require limited reforestation investments. McReynolds and Burns (1973) reported that direct seeding was a better alternative to planting and natural regeneration for this species.

In a comparison of sand, slash, and longleaf pine—planted and seeded—Outcalt (1985) found that nursery seedlings grew faster, but by age 8 years, growth of sand pine was similar on both planted and seeded areas. Planted slash and longleaf trees were still significantly larger than direct seeded trees due to the advantage gained initially. Comparisons among species found that on these sandhill sites, sand pine had the best rate of growth and was the only species successfully established by direct seeding.

To minimize costs and control spacing and stocking of seeded sand pine, Outcalt (1990) evaluated a tractor-drawn scarifier-seeder for regeneration of sand pine. Called the Bracke® seeder, this device distributes seeds along small, machine-created ridges which were about 3 inches high. This equipment has been operationally used in the sand-pine scrub ecosystem and results in successful seeded stands that are cost appropriate for the slow growth and productivity of these sites.

Shortleaf pine is another species that grows on soils of low productivity—these are mountainous and rocky, but well suited for direct seeding. Gwaze and others (2005) and Seidel and Rogers (1965) built the case for restoration of shortleaf pine which once occupied 6.6 million acres, but now is found on <400,000 acres. Much of this land is in small land ownerships and suited for relatively inexpensive

Seeding with cyclone seeders is a viable regeneration option for land managers who have small tracts to reforest. Longleaf pine seeds are being distributed by men in this photo.

Sand pine growing on infertile sandhill sites in northwest Florida. This sand pine scrub ecosystem is common on these deep, sandy sites.

direct seeding. Gwaze and others (2005) also provide guidelines for direct seeding shortleaf pine in Missouri. The authors suggest that direct seeding is a potentially viable and cost-effective method of restoring shortleaf pine.

With exception of large areas where extensive forests were destroyed by wildfire or other natural disasters, selection of species suited for direct seeding are those that typically grow on infertile soils or inaccessible sites and that may be economically reforested by direct seeding.

What are Weather Constraints?

Many have noted that arid soils or periods of low rainfall may reduce the success of direct seeding. During the late 1950s and early 1960s when seeding trials were conducted and operational seeding techniques were largely applied, the South was in a period of rainfall that favored direct seeding. In more recent years, rainfall has fallen below the averages of the 1950s and 1960s.

To evaluate current rainfall patterns to that of the period of successful direct seeding, weather data was analyzed

by the Palmer Drought Severity Index (PDSI). The PDSI is the most commonly used drought index in the United States and was developed to measure intensity, duration, and spatial extent of drought. PDSI values are derived from measurements of precipitation, air temperature, and local soil moisture, along with prior values of these measures. Values range from -6.0 (extreme drought) to +6.0 (extreme wet conditions), and have been standardized to facilitate comparisons from region to region (Palmer 1965, Thornthwaite 1948).

Based on the average monthly PDSI for the fall and winter months (October through March), the period from late 1956 through early 1962 was less droughty than for the 30-year period from late 1932 through early 1962, with the exception of February that was similarly droughty in both periods (table 2). The relatively moist era from fall 1956 through winter 1962 was when direct seeding was most widely used in central Louisiana. In addition, the period between late 1956 through early 1962 was also less droughty than from late 2006 through early 2012. In fact, the 6-year period from late 2007 through early 2012 was drier than the 30-year period from late 1982 through early 2012. This suggests that direct seeding might not have been as successful in recent years as in the past because of the sensitivity of germinating pine seeds to droughty conditions.

These data indicate that land managers and owners thinking of using direct seeding as a regeneration tool should consider the severity of soil moisture regime for the area planned for seeding. PDSI data are readily available from the NOAA National Climate Data Center Web site www. ncdc.noaa.gov/oa/climate/research/prelim/drought/palmer. html.

What Does Site Preparation Need To Accomplish?

Site preparation for direct seeding should accomplish two purposes (Ezell 2012). First, mineral soil must be exposed. This can be done by burning or disking the area if it is an old field, or the area can be disked and burned if this is the better treatment to achieve the needed result. Second, some degree of competition control is desirable. The site treatments must result in enough competition control to get a stand established and begin height growth. If economically feasible, an application of herbicides may be beneficial in areas where competing vegetation is well established and hard to control.

What Seed Treatments Are Needed?

Seed availability must be considered. Since most landowners do not have the capability to collect and process seeds, they routinely purchase from commercial seed

Table 2—Average Palmer Drought Severity Index values from fall 1956 through winter 1962, fall 2006 through winter 2012, and the preceding 30-year averages for both periods in central Louisiana (positive numbers mean wetter and negative numbers mean drier than normal)[a]

Month	Fall 1956 through winter 1962	30-year average for fall 1932– winter 1962	Fall 2006 through winter 2012	30-year average for fall 1982– winter 2012
October	0.60	-1.93	-2.58	2.14
November	0.78	-1.54	-3.76	2.77
December	1.43	-1.91	-2.80	1.13
January	0.80	-1.00	-3.09	0.67
February	-1.46	-1.21	-3.54	0.72
March	2.39	-0.15	-3.84	-0.66

[a]Average Palmer Drought Severity Index values for the 6-month periods were calculated by James D Haywood U S Department of Agriculture Forest Service Southern Research Station Pineville LA 71360

dealers. Seeds should have viability of at least 85 percent and a minimum of 95 percent sound seeds.

Two types of seed treatments may be required for successful direct seeding. The first depends on the amount of seed dormancy that may require stratification or prechilling to assure prompt germination after seeding. Most forest seed companies have the knowledge and resources to provide appropriate seed stratification treatments.

The second seed treatment is to protect the seeds from bird and rodent predation after seeding and through the germination process. Thiram is the most common bird repellent. It also provides a limited amount of rodent repellency. However, if the area to be seeded is relatively small, rodent predation can be a serious problem because animals can be drawn from surrounding areas. The best replacement for endrin is capsicum, which in combination with thiram, provides good seed protection. Effective rates for this repellent coating per pound of seed are: 76 ml thiram (Gustafson 42-S®), 3 ml latex, and 1 ml capsicum (concentration of 500,000 Soville Units).

Most forest seed companies can provide the seeds of the species needed along with necessary stratification and repellent treatments.

When Should Seeds Be Sown?

Longleaf and sand pine seeds are typically sown in the fall when soil moisture is fully recharged. Seeds of both species germinate promptly without stratification. Seed predation is normally low in the fall as rodent populations increase later in the fall and winter.

Species such as loblolly, shortleaf, and slash pine have more dormant seeds and are stratified before sowing in the early spring, about when the first redbud and red maple blooms appear. Stratified seeds sown in mid-February usually complete germination by mid-April.

Disking an area with grass sod allows seeds to become in contact with mineral soil and reduces vegetative competition after germination.

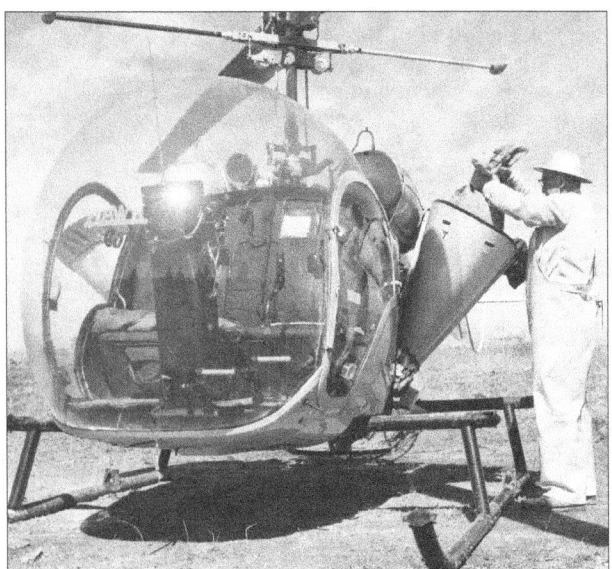

Pilot loading treated pine seeds into a seed hopper mounted on a helicopter for broadcast seeding.

How Are Seeds Distributed?

There are many methods of sowing seeds. Large tracts of land (over 500 acres) are often broadcast sown by airplanes or helicopters. This method is fast and provides accurate and complete coverage. Another method for large tracts of land uses row-seeding machines, which plow or disk a narrow furrow or strip, meter out specific amounts of seeds, and pack the seed into the soil.

Small tracts of land can be sown with hand-sowing or spot-sowing techniques. Hand-cranked cyclone seeders with metering devices are the most efficient. One person can sow 15 acres per day. Seeds can also be sown on hand-raked spots, approximately 2 feet in diameter and spaced about 8 by 8 feet (Duryea 1992). Five to 8 seeds should be pressed into the soil at each spot and 2 to 4 acres can be sown in 1 day using this method.

How Is Direct Seeding Success Determined?

Since many variables affect the success of direct seeding, careful inventories are needed to evaluate the results. At least one inventory is essential at the end of the growing season following seeding.

Sample plots should be of milacre (1/1000 of an acre) size for broadcast-seeded areas. These are circular plots with a radius 3 feet 8.7 inches. The plots can be measured using a stiff wire or stick of that length for scanning the plot area from a central point. The number of seedlings found in each plot is recorded.

Twenty-five is the minimum number of plots for any seeded area (Ezell 2012). On large areas, one plot per acre may be sufficient. To obtain the number of seedlings per acre, the following procedure is used: (1) divide the total number of counted seedlings on all plots by the number of plots, and (2) multiply the average number of seedlings by 1,000. To determine the stocking percentage, multiply the number of plots with 1 or more seedlings by 100.

A successful seeding is one that results in over 1,000 seedlings per acre with 55 percent stocking. If the inventory indicates fewer than 1,000 seedlings per acre or <55 percent stocking, make another inventory at the end of the second growing season before a decision is made on whether to reseed or plant. Areas with more than 2,000 seedlings per acre at the end of the first growing season should be resampled at the end of the third year to determine if precommercial thinning is needed.

Row seeding and spot seeding will require a different sampling approach for best accuracy, but the milacre method may be used with confidence if enough samples are taken (Mann and Derr 1964).

CONCLUSIONS

Millions of acres of cutover pine forests resulting from the "golden-age of lumbering" early in the 20th century provided a challenge to foresters. Forests in the West Gulf region were particularly decimated due to the use of steam-powered logging equipment as aggressive harvesting moved into this region. Wakeley (1930) estimated that based on the then rate of planting, it would take 900 or 1,000 years to reforest the denuded forest land that occurred throughout the Nation.

With this understanding of the need for reforestation capability, the Southern Forest Experiment Station established a research center at Alexandria, LA in 1946, with reforestation research as a priority. At the time, the capacity of tree nurseries to provide needed amounts of planting stock was limited. The idea, then, of direct seeding large acreages quickly was intriguing and became a research priority.

Early studies determined that a major limitation in successful seeding was bird and rodent predation. With collaboration of the U.S. Fish and Wildlife Service, scientists found effective repellents, and direct seeding became a possible reforestation option. Anthraquinone and thiram were found to effectively repel birds from eating pine seed and were environmentally safe chemicals. Endrin did a good job of limiting losses due to rodents,

Direct seeded longleaf pine seedlings that have begun height growth. Direct seeding was used to effectively reforest hundreds of thousands of acres with longleaf pine.

but after numerous years of use was withdrawn from the market due to environmental concerns. However, use of the thiram-endrin combination resulted in successful direct seeding and was used across the South and beyond. More recently, endrin was replaced with capsicum, which lacks the level of protection of endrin, but in combination with thiram does provide a good level of seed protection.

The practice of direct seeding proved applicable throughout the South. The dramatic development and use of direct seeding caused the need for expanding supporting research in seed science, in control of undesired and low-quality hardwoods on many pine sites, and in determination of site preparation needed for successful seeding.

The development of direct seeding and the related research programs at Alexandria gained national and international recognition. In 1961, the Alexandria Research Center was awarded the U.S. Department of Agriculture Superior Service Award for these research accomplishments.

By the early 1970s, direct seeding had been highly effective in restoring southern pines to almost 2 million acres of cutover forest land throughout the South. As much of the open forest land was reforested by planting

and seeding, the need for direct seeding declined. Use of seeding is most efficient on large, open areas. Loss of the availability of endrin, the effective rodent repellent, further limited the application of seeding. Too, the lack of stocking control with seeding often resulted in excessively stocked stands that required precommercial thinning. With the capacity of forest tree nurseries greatly increasing the use of genetically improved seeds, planting became the most attractive option on highly productive forest land. For these reasons, use of direct seeding continued to decline.

Currently, the use of direct seeding is primarily limited to restoration of large forested areas destroyed by wildfires or other natural disasters and to areas of low soil productivity where it is not economically feasible to plant more expensive nursery stock. Seeding is also a viable alternative for land ownerships where small tracts need reforestation. The economics of seeding on such areas make direct seeding a good option.

For seeding to be a practical alternative technique, even on favorable sites, a high degree of technical skill and knowledge is needed. The key to success lies in obtaining the advice and assistance of an experienced specialist. Unfortunately, the availability of such specialists is now limited, and for this reason use of direct seeding may continue to decline.

Before direct seeding their land, land managers and owners should consider the severity of the drought index for the area planned for seeding. If soils are droughty, the success of direct seeding operations may be significantly reduced.

Regardless of future use, direct seeding was developed and applied to meet a specific need—reforestation of massive areas of cutover forest land. Seeding technology was developed over a few years and was put in use immediately. This was a remarkable accomplishment and resulted from intensive collaboration among Forest Service research scientists, U.S. Fish and Wildlife Service, forest industry operational managers, and university extension specialists. Direct seeding met a significant need at the time—millions of acres of devastated forest land were put into production.

W.F. William "Bill" Mann, Jr. (left), leader of the research program, is shown receiving the U.S. Department of Agriculture Superior Service Award from Carl Ostrum (right) of the Forest Service's Washington Office. Harold D. Burkhalter (center) represents the Louisiana Forestry Association, a major supporter of the research program.

ACKNOWLEDGMENTS

The scientists who worked to develop direct seeding technology were dedicated and determined. Their contributions were recognized through the numerous publications that chronicled their research. This document is dedicated to those technical support personnel who spent their careers supporting the research efforts and who contributed significantly— without recognition—to the success of the programs.

LITERATURE CITED

American Spice Trade Association. 1960. Official analytical methods of the American Spice Trade Association. New York: American Spice Trade Association. 45 p.

Barnett, J.P. 1964. Stored longleaf seed successfully direct seeded. Tree Planters' Notes. 65: 3-5.

Barnett, J.P. 1969. Long-term storage of longleaf pine seeds. Tree Planters' Notes. 20(2): 22-25.

Barnett, J.P. 1971. Aerated water soaks stimulate germination of southern pine seeds. Res. Pap. SO-67. New Orleans: U.S. Department of Agriculture Forest Service, Southern Forest Experiment Station. 9 p.

Barnett, J.P. 1972. Seedcoat influences dormancy of loblolly pine seeds. Canadian Journal of Forest Research. 2: 7-10.

Barnett, J.P. 1976a. Cone and seed maturation of southern pines. Res. Pap. SO-122. New Orleans: U.S. Department of Agriculture Forest Service, Southern Forest Experiment Station. 11 p.

Barnett, J.P. 1976b. Delayed germination of southern pine seeds related to seed coat constraint. Canadian Journal of Forest Research. 6: 504-510.

Barnett, J.P. 1976c. Sterilizing southern pine seeds with hydrogen peroxide. Tree Planters' Notes. 27(3): 17-19.

Barnett, J.P. 1979a. An easy way to measure cone specific gravity. In: Karrfalt, R.P., comp. Proceedings, Seed Collection Workshop, 1979 May 16-18; Macon, GA. Tech. Publ. SA-TP 8. Atlanta, GA: U.S. Department of Agriculture Forest Service, State and Private Forestry: 21-23.

Barnett, J.P. 1979b. Southern pine cone maturation and storage. In: Karrfalt, R.P., comp. Proceedings, Seed Collection Workshop; 1979 May 16-18; Macon, GA. Tech. Publ. SA-TP 8. Atlanta, GA: U.S. Department of Agriculture Forest Service, State and Private Forestry: 11-20.

Barnett, J.P. 1991. Relating the seed coat of *Pinus* to speed of germination, geographic variation, and seedling development. In: Proceedings, twenty-first southern forest tree improvement conference; 1991 June 17-20; Knoxville, TN. Knoxville, TN: The Southern Forest Tree Improvement Committee in cooperation with The University of Tennessee and Tennessee Division of Forestry: 266-275.

Barnett, J.P. 1995. Anipel fails to repel rodents from direct seeded longleaf pine seeds. In: Edwards, M.B., comp. Proceedings of the eighth biennial southern silvicultural research conference. Gen. Tech. Rep. SRS-1. Asheville, NC: U.S. Department of Agriculture Forest Service, Southern Research Station: 119-121.

Barnett, J.P. 1996. Longleaf pine seed quality: can it be improved? In: Landis, T.D.; South, D.B., tech. coords. National proceedings, Forest and Conservation Nursery Associations. Gen. Tech. Rep. PNW-GTR-389. Portland, OR: U.S. Department of Agriculture Forest Service, Pacific Northwest Research Station: 69-74.

Barnett, J.P. 1998. Oleoresin capsicum has potential as a rodent repellent in direct seeding longleaf pine. In: Waldrop, T.A., ed. Proceedings of the ninth biennial southern silvicultural research conference. Gen. Tech. Rep. SRS-20. Asheville, NC: U.S. Department of Agriculture Forest Service, Southern Research Station: 326-328.

Barnett, J.P. 1999. Guidelines for estimating cone and seed yields of southern pines. In: Proceedings, Twenty-fifth biennial southern forest tree improvement conference; 1999 July 10-14; New Orleans, LA. Sponsored publication 47. Baton Rouge, LA: Southern Forest Tree Improvement Committee: 31-35.

Barnett, J.P. 2011. Faces from the past: profiles of those who led restoration of the South's forests. Gen. Tech. Rep. SRS-133. Asheville, NC: U.S. Department of Agriculture Forest Service, Southern Research Station. 68 p.

Barnett, J.P.; Bergman, P.W.; Ferguson, W.L. [and others]. 1977. The biologic and economic assessment of endrin: a report of the endrin assessment team to the rebuttable presumption against registration of endrin. Tech. Bull. 1623. Washington, DC: U.S. Department of Agriculture. 47 p.

Barnett, J.; Burns, A. 2011. Delaneys of Woodworth: innovative forestry for decades. Forests & People. 61(4): 14-16.

Barnett, J.P.; Haywood, J.D.; Pearson, H.A. 2011. Louisiana's Palustris Experimental Forest: 75 years of research that transformed the South. Gen. Tech. Rep. SRS-148. Asheville, NC: U.S. Department of Agriculture Forest Service, Southern Research Station. 64 p.

Barnett, J.P.; Jones, J.P. 1993. Response of longleaf pine seeds to storage conditions and pregermination treatments. Southern Journal of Applied Forestry. 17: 180-187.

Barnett, J.P.; McGilvray, J.M. 1997. Practical guidelines for producing longleaf pine seedlings in containers. Gen. Tech. Rep. SRS-14. Asheville, NC: U.S. Department of Agriculture Forest Service, Southern Research Station. 36 p.

Barnett, J.P.; McGilvary, J.M. 2002. Guidelines for producing quality longleaf pine seeds. Gen. Tech. Rep. SRS-52. Asheville, NC: U.S. Department of Agriculture Forest Service, Southern Research Station. 21 p.

Barnett, J.P.; McLemore, B.F. 1966. Repellent-coated pine seed can be stored. Forest Farmer. 25(9): 14.

Barnett, J.P.; McLemore, B.F. 1970. Storing southern pine seeds. Journal of Forestry. 68: 24-27.

Barnett, J.P.; Pesacreta, T.C. 1993. Handling longleaf pine seeds for optimal nursery performance. Southern Journal of Applied Forestry. 17: 174-179.

Barnett, J.P.; Vozzo, J.A. 1985. Viability and vigor of slash and shortleaf pine seeds after 50 years of storage. Forest Science. 31: 316-320.

Boggs, J.A.; Wittwer, R.F. 1993. Emergence and establishment of shortleaf pine under various seedbed conditions. Southern Journal of Applied Forestry. 17(1): 44-48.

Bonner, F.T. 1987. Cone storage and seed quality in longleaf pine. Res. Note SO-341. New Orleans: U.S. Department of Agriculture Forest Service, Southern Forest Experiment Station. 4 p.

Bramlett, D.L.; Hutchinson, J.G. 1964. Estimating sound seed per cone in shortleaf pine. Res. Note SE-18. Asheville, NC: U.S. Department of Agriculture Forest Service, Southeastern Forest Experiment Station. 2 p.

Brissette, J.C.; Barnett, J.P. 1989. Depth of planting and J-rooting affect loblolly pine seedlings under stress conditions. In: Miller, J.H., comp. Proceedings of the fifth biennial southern silvicultural research conference. Gen. Tech. Rep. SO-74. New Orleans: U.S. Department of Agriculture Forest Service, Southern Forest Experiment Station: 155-158.

Burleigh, T.D. 1938. The relation of birds to the establishment of longleaf pine seedlings in southern Mississippi. Occasional Paper 75. New Orleans: U.S. Department of Agriculture Forest Service, Southern Forest Experiment Station. 5 p.

Burns, R.M. 1961. Seed sowing tools. Tree Planters' Notes. 45: 3-4.

Campbell, T.E. 1975. Yields of direct seeded loblolly pine at age 22 years. Res. Note SO-199. New Orleans: U.S. Department of Agriculture Forest Service, Southern Forest Experiment Station. 3 p.

Campbell, T.E. 1981a. The effects of endrin in repellent seed coverings on caged rodents. Res. Pap. SO-174. New Orleans: U.S. Department of Agriculture Forest Service, Southern Forest Experiment Station. 4 p

Campbell, T.E. 1981b. Spot seeding is effective and inexpensive for reforesting small acreages. In: Barnett, J.P., ed. First biennial southern silvicultural research conference. Gen. Tech. Rep. SO-34. U.S. Department of Agriculture Forest Service, Southern Forest Experiment Station: 88-91.

Campbell, T.E. 1981c. Growth and development of loblolly and slash pines direct-seeded or planted on a cutover site. Southern Journal of Applied Forestry. 5(3): 115-119.

Campbell, T.E. 1982a. Direct seeding may present attractive option for pine regeneration on smaller tracts. Forest Farmer. XLII(2): 8-9, 26.

Campbell, T.E. 1982b. Guidelines for direct seeding. In: Jordan, F.; Balmer, W.E., eds. How to help landowners with forest regeneration. Atlanta, GA: U.S. Department of Agriculture Forest Service, Southeastern Region, State and Private Forestry: 20-26.

Campbell, T.E. 1985a. Development of direct-seeded and planted loblolly and slash pines through age 20. Southern Journal of Applied Forestry. 9(10): 205-211.

Campbell, T.E. 1985b. Sprouting of slash, loblolly, and shortleaf pines following a simulated precommercial thinning. Res. Note SO-320. New Orleans: U.S. Department of Agriculture Forest Service, Southern Forest Experiment Station. 3 p.

Cao, Q.V.; Baldwin, V.C., Jr.; Lohrey, R.E. 1997. Site index curves for direct-seeded loblolly and longleaf pines in Louisiana. Southern Journal of Applied Forestry. 21(3): 134-138.

Cassady, J.T.; Mann, W.F., Jr. 1954. The Alexandria Research Center. New Orleans: U.S. Department of Agriculture Forest Service, Southern Forest Experiment Station. 49 p.

Croker, T.C. 1971. Binocular counts of longleaf pine strobili. Res. Pap. SO-127. New Orleans: U.S. Department of Agriculture Forest Service, Southern Forest Experiment Station. 2 p.

Derr, H.J. 1958. Direct seeding: a fast, reliable method of regenerating longleaf pine. Tree Planters' Notes. 32: 15-20.

Derr, H.J. 1964. New repellent formulation for direct seeding. Journal of Forestry. 62(4): 265.

Derr, H.J.; Mann, W.F., Jr. 1959. Guidelines for direct-seeding longleaf pine. Occasional Paper 171. New Orleans: U.S. Department of Agriculture Forest Service, Southern Forest Experiment Station. 22 p.

Derr, H.J.; Mann, W.F., Jr. 1971. Direct-seeding pines in the South. Agric. Handb. 391. Washington, DC: U.S. Department of Agriculture Forest Service. 69 p.

Derr, H.J.; Mann, W.F., Jr. 1977. Bedding poorly drained sites for planting loblolly and slash pines. Res. Pap. SO-134. New Orleans: U.S. Department of Agriculture Forest Service, Southern Forest Experiment Station. 4 p.

Duryea, M.L. 1992. Forest regeneration methods: natural regeneration, direct seeding and planting. Circular 759. Gainesville, FL: University of Florida, Florida Cooperative Extension Service, Institute of Food and Agricultural Sciences. 13 p.

Ezell, A.W. 2012. Direct seeding, a forest regeneration alternative. Publication 1588. Starkville, MS: Mississippi State University, Department of Forestry. http://msucares.com/pubs/publications/p1588.htm. [Date accessed: December 18, 2012].

Fatzinger, C.W.; Muse, H.D.; Miller, T.; Bhattacharyya, H.T. 1988. Estimating cone and seed production and monitoring pest damage in southern pine seed orchards. Res. Pap. SE-271. Asheville, NC: U.S. Department of Agriculture Forest Service, Southeastern Forest Experiment Station. 30 p.

Fox, W.; Smith, E.A.; Lohrey, R.E. 1976. Precommercial thinning—the worth. In: Proceedings national silvicultural conference, Oct. 13-15, 1976, Eugene, WA. Beltsville, MD: Society of American Foresters: 161-168.

Grelen, H.E. 1975. Vegetative response to twelve years of seasonal burning on a Louisiana longleaf pine site. Res. Note SO-192. New Orleans: U.S. Department of Agriculture Forest Service, Southern Forest Experiment Station. 4 p.

Grelen, H.E. 1983. May burning favors survival and early height growth of longleaf pine seedlings. Southern Journal of Applied Forestry. 7: 16-19.

Gwaze, D.; Henken, D.; Johanson, M. 2005. Direct seeding of shortleaf pine (Pinus echinata Mill.): a review. Forest Research Report 5. Columbia, MO: Missouri Department of Conservation. 16 p.

Hatchell, G.E. 1966. Loblolly pine direct seeding in the lower Piedmont of Georgia. Res. Pap. 40. Macon, GA: Georgia Forest Research Council. 4 p.

Haywood, J.D. 1983. Response of planted pines to site preparation on a Beauregard-Caddo soil. In: Jones, E.P., Jr., ed. Proceedings second biennial southern silvicultural research conference. Gen. Tech. Rep. SE-24. Asheville, NC: U.S. Department of Agriculture Forest Service, Southeastern Forest Experiment Station: 14-17.

Haywood, J.D.; Barnett, J.P. 1994. Comparing methods of artificially regenerating loblolly and slash pines: container planting, bareroot planting, and spot seeding. Tree Planters' Notes. 45(2): 63-67.

Harrington, C.A.; Carlson, W.C.; Brissette, J.C. 1986. Relationships between height growth and root system orientation in planted and seeded loblolly and shortleaf pines. In: Phillips, D.R., comp. Proceedings of the fourth biennial southern silvicultural research conference. Gen. Tech. Rep. SE-42. Asheville, NC: U.S. Department of Agriculture Forest Service, Southeastern Forest Experiment Station: 53-60.

Hodges, J.D.; Scheer, R.L. 1962. Soil cover aids germination of pine seed on sandy sites. Tree Planters' Notes. 54: 1-3.

Hoffman, P.G.; Lego, M.C. 1983. Separation and quantitation of red-pepper major heat principles by reverse-phase high-pressure liquid chromatography. Journal of Agricultural Food Chemistry. 31: 1326-1330.

Hopkins, D.R. 1956. The Osborne tree cone cutting knife. Journal of Forestry. 54: 534.

Jarvis, W.T.; Beers, W.L. 1965. Reclamation of a wasteland in Central Gulf Coastal Plain. Journal of Forestry. 63: 3-7.

Jones, L. 1963. A test of direct seeding depths for slash and longleaf pine. Res. Note SE-5. Asheville, NC: U.S. Department of Agriculture Forest Service, Southeastern Forest Experiment Station. 2 p.

Karrfalt, R.P. 1988. Stratification of longleaf pine. In: Lantz, C.W., ed. Proceedings, Southern Forest Nursery Association Meeting; 1988 July 25-28; Charleston, SC. Columbia, SC: Southern Forest Nursery Association: 46-48.

Lohrey, R.E. 1970. Spot seeding slash and loblolly pines. Forest Farmer. 29(12): 12, 18.

Lohrey, R.E. 1972. Precommercial thinning of direct-seeded loblolly pine. Res. Note SO-139. New Orleans: U.S. Department of Agriculture Forest Service, Southern Forest Experiment Station. 4 p.

Lohrey, R.E. 1973a. Planted pines grow better than seeded pines on hardwood-dominated site. Tree Planters' Notes. 24(2): 12-13.

Lohrey, R.E. 1973b. Precommercial thinning increases diameter and height growth of slash pine. Res. Note SO-152. New Orleans: U.S. Department of Agriculture Forest Service, Southern Forest Experiment Station. 4 p.

Lohrey, R.E. 1974. Site preparation improves survival and growth of direct-seeded pines. Res. Note SO-185. New Orleans: U.S. Department of Agriculture Forest Service, Southern Forest Experiment Station. 4 p.

Lohrey, R.E. 1977. Growth responses of loblolly pine to commercial thinning. Southern Journal of Applied Forestry. 1: 19-22.

Lohrey, R.E. 1984. Aboveground biomass of planted and direct-seeded slash pine in the West Gulf Region. In: Saucier, J.R., ed. Proceedings of the 1984 Southern Forest Biomass Workshop. Athens, GA: University of Georgia, School of Forest Resources; Asheville, NC: U.S. Department of Agriculture Forest Service, Southeastern Forest Experiment Station: 75-82.

Lohrey, R.E. 1987. Site index curves for direct-seeded slash pine in Louisiana. Southern Journal of Applied Forestry. 11: 15-17.

Lohrey, R.E.; Jones, E.P., Jr. 1983. Natural regeneration and direct seeding. In: Stone, E.L., ed. Proceedings of the managed slash pine ecosystem symposium. Gainesville, FL: University of Florida, School of Forest Resources: 183-193.

McKee, W.H., Jr.; Shoulders, E. 1970. Depth of water table and redox potential of soil affect slash pine growth. Forest Science. 16: 399-401.

McKee, W.H., Jr.; Shoulders, E. 1974. Slash pine biomass response to site preparation and soil properties. Soil Science Society of America Proceedings. 38(1): 144-148.

McLemore, B.F. 1959. Cone maturity affects germination of longleaf pine seed. Journal of Forestry. 57: 648-650.

McLemore, B.F. 1961a. Estimating pine seed yields. Southern Forestry Notes 134. New Orleans: U.S. Department of Agriculture Forest Service, Southern Forest Experiment Station. [Not paged].

McLemore, B.F. 1961b. Prolonged storage of longleaf cones weakens seed. Southern Forestry Notes 132. New Orleans: U.S. Department of Agriculture, Forest Service, Southern Forest Experiment Station. [Not paged].

McLemore, B.F. 1961c. Storage of longleaf pine seed. Tree Planters' Notes. 47: 15-19.

McLemore, B.F. 1962. Predicting seed yields of southern pine cones. Journal of Forestry. 60: 639-641.

McLemore, B.F. 1965. Pentane flotation for separating full and empty longleaf pine seeds. Forest Science. 11: 242-243.

McLemore, B.F. 1975. Collection date, cone-storage period affect southern pine seed yields. Tree Planters' Notes. 26(1): 24-26.

McLemore, B.F.; Barnett, J.P. 1966. Storing repellent-coated southern pine seed. Journal of Forestry. 64: 619-621.

McLemore, B.F.; Czabator, F.J. 1961. Length of stratification and germination of loblolly pine seed. Journal of Forestry. 59: 267-269.

McReynolds, R.D. 1960. Mortality of newly germinated southern pine seedlings following inundation. Tree Planters' Notes. 43: 23-25.

McReynolds, R.D.; Burns, R.M. 1973. Direct seeding sand pines in the sandhills of northwest Florida. In: Proceedings of the sand pine symposium. Gen. Tech. Rep. SE-2. Asheville, NC: U.S. Department of Agriculture Forest Service, Southeastern Forest Experiment Station: 107-115.

Mann, W.F., Jr. 1956. Direct-seeding the southern pines. Tree Planters' Notes. 25: 12-19.

Mann, W.F., Jr. 1958. Guides for direct seeding the southern pines. Forests & People. 8(2): 16-17, 47-50.

Mann, W.F., Jr. 1959. Preparing seed for direct seeding. In: Woods, F.W., ed. Direct seeding in the South, 1959. A symposium. Durham, NC: Duke University, School of Forestry: 52-61.

Mann, W.F., Jr. 1962. Tools for direct seeding. Forest Farmer. 21(5): 13-16.

Mann, W.F., Jr. 1965. Progress in seeding the southern pines. In: Abbott, H.G., ed. Proceedings symposium on direct seeding in the Northeast; August 25-27, 1964. Amherst, MA: University of Massachusetts: 9-13.

Mann, W.F., Jr. 1968. Ten years' experience with direct seeding in the South. Journal of Forestry. 66(11): 828-833.

Mann, W.F., Jr. 1969. A review—techniques and progress in regenerating southern pines. Forest Products Journal. 19(8): 10-16.

Mann, W.F., Jr. 1970. Direct-seeding longleaf pine. Res. Pap. SO-57. New Orleans: U.S. Department of Agriculture Forest Service, Southern Forest Experiment Station. 26 p.

Mann, W.F., Jr.; Burkhalter, H.D. 1961. The South's largest successful direct seeding. Journal of Forestry. 59(2): 83-87.

Mann, W.F., Jr.; Burns, E.B. 1965. Direct seeding for the small landowner. Forest Farmer. 25(3): 6-7, 14.

Mann, W.F., Jr.; Derr, H.J. 1955. Not for the birds. Tree Planters' Notes. 20: 3-6.

Mann, W.F., Jr.; Derr, H.J. 1961. Guidelines for direct-seeding loblolly pine. Occasional Paper 188. New Orleans: U.S. Department of Agriculture Forest Service, Southern Forest Experiment Station. 23 p.

Mann, W.F., Jr.; Derr, H.J. 1964. Guides for direct-seeding slash pine. Res. Pap. SO-12. New Orleans; U.S. Department of Agriculture Forest Service, Southern Forest Experiment Station. 27 p.

Mann, W.F., Jr.; Derr, H.J. 1970. Response of planted loblolly and slash pine to disking on a poorly drained site. Res. Note SO-110. New Orleans: U.S. Department of Agriculture Forest Service, Southern Forest Experiment Station. 3 p.

Mann, W.F., Jr.; Derr, H.J.; Meanley, B. 1956. Bird repellents for direct seeding longleaf pine. Forests & People. 6(3): 16-17, 48.

Mann, W.F., Jr.; Lohrey, R.E. 1974. Precommercial thinning of southern pines. Journal of Forestry. 72: 557-560.

Meanley, B.; Mann, W.F., Jr.; Derr, H.J. 1957. New bird repellents for longleaf seed. Tree Planters' Notes. 28: 8.

Miller, S.R. 1957. Germination of slash pine seed following submergence in water. Woodland Research Notes 3. Savannah, SC: Union Bag-Camp Paper Company. 2 p.

Nolte, D.L.; Barnett, J.P. 2000. A repellent to reduce mouse damage to longleaf pine seed. International Biodeterioration & Biodegradation. 45: 169-174.

Outcalt, K.W. 1985. Direct seeding versus planting for establishment of pines on west Florida sandhills. In: Shoulders, E., ed. Proceedings of the third biennial southern silvicultural research conference. Gen. Tech. Rep. SO-54. New Orleans: U.S. Department of Agriculture Forest Service, Southern Forest Experiment Station: 122-124.

Outcalt, K.W. 1990. Operational trials of a scarifier-seeder for regenerating Ocala sand pine. Southern Journal of Applied Forestry. 14: 85-88.

Palmer, W.C. 1965. Meteorological drought. Res. Pap. 45. Washington, DC; Weather Bureau, Office of Climatology. 58 p.

Pawuk, W.H. 1978. Damping-off of container-grown longleaf pine seedlings by seedborne *Fusaria*. Plant Disease Reporter. 62: 82-84.

Peevy, F.A. 1947. Killing undesirable hardwoods with herbicides. Southern Lumberman. 175(2201): 123-125.

Peevy, F.A. 1960. Controlling southern weed trees with herbicides. Journal of Forestry. 58(9): 708-710.

Peevy, F.A. 1961. Control of blackjack oak by basal spraying of 2,4,5-T. Weeds. 9(1): 50-53.

Peevy, F.A.; Burns, P.Y. 1959. Effectiveness of aerial application of herbicides for hardwood control in Louisiana. Weeds. 7(4): 463-469.

Richardson, B.Y. 1965. New tools for direct seeding. Southern Lumberman. 211(2632): 150-151.

Rietveld, W.J.; Heidmann, L.J. 1976. Direct seeding ponderosa pine on recent burns in Arizona. Res. Note RM-312. Fort Collins, CO: U.S. Department of Agriculture Forest Service, Rocky Mountain Forest and Range Experiment Station. 8 p.

Russell, T.E.; Rhame, T.E. 1961. The advantages of disking for slash pine. Forests & People. 11(1): 12-13.

Schmidtling, R.C. 2001. Southern pine seed sources. Gen. Tech. Rep. SRS-44. Asheville, NC: U.S. Department of Agriculture Forest Service, Southern Research Station. 25 p.

Seidel, K.W.; Rogers, N.F. 1965. Seeding shortleaf pine in the Missouri Ozarks. Res. Pap. CS-21. Columbus, OH: U.S. Department of Agriculture Forest Service, Central States Forest Experiment Station. 12 p.

Shipman, R.D. 1963. Seeding depth—its influence on establishment of direct-seeded pine in the South Carolina sandhills. Journal of Forestry. 61: 907-912.

Shoulders, E. 1968. Fertilization increases longleaf and slash pine flower and cone crops in Louisiana. Journal of Forestry. 66: 192-197.

Shoulders, E.; McKee, W.H., Jr. 1973. Pine nutrition in the West Gulf Coastal Plain: a status report. Gen. Tech. Rep. SO-2. New Orleans: U.S. Department of Agriculture Forest Service, Southern Forest Experiment Station. 26 p.

Shoulders, E.; Tiarks, A.E. 1980. Predicting height and relative performance of major southern pines from rainfall, slope, and available soil moisture. Forest Science. 26(3): 437-447.

Syverson, M.L. 1960. Cone cutter. Tree Planters' Notes. 42: 1-2.

Thornthwaite, C.W. 1948. An approach toward a rational classification of climate. Geographical Review. 38: 55–94.

Tiarks, A.E.; Haywood, J.D. 1981. Response of newly established slash pine to cultivation and fertilization. Res. Note SO-272. New Orleans: U.S. Department of Agriculture Forest Service, Southern Forest Experiment Station. 4 p.

Vietmeyer, N.D. 1981. Sowing forests from the air: report of an ad hoc panel of the advisory committee on technology innovation, Board on Science and Technology for International Development, National Research Council. Washington, DC: National Academy Press. 61 p.

Wakeley, P.C. 1930. Fitting forest planting to American needs. Journal of Forestry. 28(4): 500-503.

Wakeley, P.C. 1954. Planting the southern pines. Agricultural Monograph 18. Washington, DC: U.S. Department of Agriculture Forest Service. 233 p.

Wakeley, P.C. 1976. F.O. "Red" Bateman, pioneer silviculturist. Journal of Forest History. 20(2): 91-99.

Wakeley, P.C.; Barnett, J.P. 1968. Viability of slash and shortleaf pine seed stored for 35 years. Journal of Forestry. 66: 840-841.

Walters, G.A.; Whitesell, C.D. 1971. Direct seeding trials of three major timber species in Hawaii. Res. Note PSW-234. Berkeley, CA: U.S. Department of Agriculture Forest Service, Pacific Southwest Forest and Range Experiment Station. 2 p.

Wasser, R.G.; Dierauf, T.A. 1979. Predicting loblolly seed orchard cone crops by means of summer binocular counts. In: Karrfalt, R.P., comp. Proceedings of the seed collection workshop: 1979 May 16-18; Macon, GA. Tech. Publ. SA-TP 8. Atlanta, GA: U.S. Department of Agriculture Forest Service, Southeastern Area, State and Private Forestry: 35-42.

Webb, C.D.; Hunt, D.L. 1965. Seed crop estimation in a slash pine production area. Res. Pap. 38. Macon, GA: Georgia Forest Research Council. 6 p.

Wells, O.O. 1969. Results of the southwide pine seed source study through 1968-69. In: Proceedings, tenth southern conference on forest tree improvement, June 17-19, 1969, Houston, TX. Sponsored Publication 30. Macon, GA: Southern Forest Tree Improvement Committee: 117-129.

Wenger, K.F. 1953. How to estimate the number of cones in standing loblolly pine trees. Res. Note 44. Asheville, NC: U.S. Department of Agriculture Forest Service, Southeastern Forest Experiment Station. 2 p.

Wheeler, P.R.; Cassady, J.T. 1956. The hardwood control job on Louisiana's pinelands. Forests & People. 6(2): 22-23, 45.

Williams, R.A.; Bohn, K.; McKeithen, J.; Demers, C. 2008. Pre-commercial thinning of loblolly pine—does it pay? For 188. Gainesville, FL: University of Florida, Institute of Food and Agricultural Sciences, Florida Cooperative Extension Service, School of Forest Resources and Conservation Department. 6 p.

Williston, H.L.; Balmer, W.E.; Tomczak, D. 1998. Managing the family forest in the South. Management Bulletin R8-MB-1. Atlanta, GA: U.S. Department of Agriculture Forest Service, Southern Region. 92 p.

Barnett, J.P. 2014. Direct seeding southern pines: history and status of a technique developed for restoring cutover forests. Gen. Tech. Rep. SRS-187. Asheville, NC: U.S. Department of Agriculture Forest Service, Southern Research Station. 35 p.

Early in the 20th century the deforestation resulting from the "golden-age of lumbering" left millions of acres of forest land in the need for reforestation. The challenge was so extreme that foresters of the early 1930s estimated that it would take 900 to 1,000 years at the then rate of planting to reforest the denuded forest land that occurred throughout the Nation. Forests of the West Gulf region were especially decimated due to the development and use of steam-powered logging equipment that left little capability for natural regeneration. Faced with this need, scientists of the Southern Forest Experiment Station began an effort to develop direct seeding with the hope of quickly seeding large open areas of the South with southern pines. Protecting seeds from bird and rodent predation was key to successful direct seeding, and in the mid-1950s certain chemicals were found that made seeding an effective tool. Additional components of a successful direct seeding operation were increasing the availability of quality pine seeds, finding methods of eliminating hardwood brush competition, and developing site preparation treatments that favored seeding. This supporting research was essential for the resulting successful restoration of millions of acres of southern pine forests. Today, direct seeding is infrequently used, primarily due to lack of large, open areas needing reforestation. But back then, seeding met a significant need, and millions of acres of forest land were put back into production.

Keywords: Chemical hardwood control, competition control, precommercial thinning, reforestation, seed repellents, seed research, site preparation, southern pines, stand stocking.

 **How do you rate this publication?**

Scan this code to submit your feedback or go to www.srs.fs.usda.gov/pubeval

Non-Discrimination Policy

The U.S. Department of Agriculture (USDA) prohibits discrimination against its customers, employees, and applicants for employment on the bases of race, color, national origin, age, disability, sex, gender identity, religion, reprisal, and where applicable, political beliefs, marital status, familial or parental status, sexual orientation, or all or part of an individual's income is derived from any public assistance program, or protected genetic information in employment or in any program or activity conducted or funded by the Department. (Not all prohibited bases will apply to all programs and/or employment activities.)

To File an Employment Complaint

If you wish to file an employment complaint, you must contact your agency's EEO Counselor (click the hyperlink for list of EEO Counselors) within 45 days of the date of the alleged discriminatory act, event, or in the case of a personnel action. Additional information can be found online at http://www.ascr.usda.gov/complaint_filing_file.html.

To File a Program Complaint

If you wish to file a Civil Rights program complaint of discrimination, complete the USDA Program Discrimination Complaint Form, found online at http://www.ascr.usda.gov/complaint_filing_cust. html, or at any USDA office, or call (866) 632-9992 to request the form. You may also write a letter containing all of the information requested in the form. Send your completed complaint form or letter to us by mail at U.S. Department of Agriculture, Director, Office of Adjudication, 1400 Independence Avenue, S.W., Washington, D.C. 20250-99410, by fax (202) 690-7442 or email at program.intake@ usda.gov.

Persons with Disabilities

Individuals who are deaf, hard of hearing or have speech disabilities and you wish to file either an EEO or program complaint please contact USDA through the Federal Relay Service at (800) 877-8339 or (800) 845-6136 (in Spanish).

Persons with disabilities who wish to file a program complaint, please see information above on how to contact us by mail directly or by email. If you require alternative means of communication for program information (e.g., Braille, large print, audiotape, etc.) please contact USDA's TARGET Center at (202) 720-2600 (voice and TDD).